Surprised

by the

Holy Spirit

There Is More for You
Than You Think

edgar mayer

EVANGELISTA MEDIA™ srl
Via Maiella, 1
66020 San Giovanni Teatino (Ch) – Italy

"Changing the World, One Book at a Time."

This book and all other Evangelista Media™ and Destiny Image™ Europe books are available at Christian bookstores and distributors worldwide.

To order products, or for any other correspondence:

EVANGELISTA MEDIA™ srl
Via della Scafa, 29/14
65013 Città Sant'Angelo – Italy
Tel. +39 085 4716623 • Fax: +39 085 9090113
Email: info@evangelistamedia.com
Or reach us on the Internet: www.evangelistamedia.com

ISBN 13: 978-88-97896-25-8
ISBN 13 EBOOK: 978-88-97896-26-5

For Worldwide Distribution, Printed in South Korea
1 2 3 4 5 6 / 15 14 13 12

Dedication

Dedicated to Tatjana Georgette,
and our daughters, Dominique and Francisca.

Contents

Foreword

When Edgar Mayer drove up on his motorbike in front of our motel room, I could never have dreamt what depth and yet childlike faith was in the man who parked his bike. He was smiling and walked over to greet us. There was something different about him. Maybe it was the gentle way with which he conducted himself or maybe it was the sparkle in his eyes, clearly to be seen as a man who loves the Holy Spirit of God. I could not put my finger on it, but I knew here stood an extraordinary man before me. This was not the first time I met him. No, our roads had crossed several times before, and every time I was impressed by the humility, yet openness for the things of the Spirit, that radiated from this man.

Edgar Mayer had studied theology as a Lutheran in Australia and Germany and yet experienced the most amazing manifestations in his church that others long and pray for. However, it was when I held the manuscript of this new book, *Surprised by the Holy Spirit,* in my hands that I knew I was in for more than a treat. This was going to be a classic. I could hardly put it down. Sometimes I looked up the Scripture passages and theology clearly stated, and at other times I actually laughed out loud, enjoying some of the humorous ways in which God dealt with him, preparing and bringing him to renewal and an amazing outpouring of the Spirit in his church.

When I read the following statement, I knew that I just had to read this book: "As it happened, my hunger and desperation for God were greater than any feelings of caution, and to be precise, the Spirit came to me and our congregation not so much as the result of an active search but divine intervention. God took us by surprise."

This book will take you on a journey that is much more than theology, though it clarifies the theology in an excellent way. It will take you into the depth and excitement of an adventure with the Holy Spirit that is remarkable. It will spark within you a hunger for more of the Holy Spirit and certainly leave you with a clear impression of what can happen to the heart and a church that starts seeking for more of God and His Holy Spirit.

I not only recommend this book, I, if at all possible, urge you to read it and let God inspire you into new dimensions in God. Be ready for a few surprises in this book that might confront your way of thinking; but also be ready for the wonderful and exciting way that God might open your life for a fresh move of the Spirit in your life and church.

Welcome to the adventure of *Surprised by the Holy Spirit—There Is More for You Than You Think!*

Suzette Hattingh, Evangelist
Founder, Voice in the City

Introduction

After almost nine years of full-time study, three theological degrees, a published thesis, and six years of parish experience in a mainline church, I should have been in a good place—but I was not. All my learning did not satisfy my hunger for God. I was hoping for more, and there was more. This book is the result of what God did in the life of our congregation and at home in our family. He surprised us with the Holy Spirit and experiences that were promised in the Bible but never understood by me.

Jesus had confirmed to His disciples that they would be "baptized with the Holy Spirit" (Acts 1:5). When this finally happened to them on the day of Pentecost, the disciples explained that the same gift of the Holy Spirit was now available to every new believer (see Acts 2:38-39). The Bible account was not complicated; therefore, the basic Christian experience of the Holy Spirit should have been familiar to me as a Bible preacher—but it was not.

At first, I had many questions and found the whole subject matter rather confusing. Every book seemed to come from a different angle, and I could not put all the pieces together. My suspicion is that others share my initial confusion. Thus, I have attempted to explain from the Bible what it means to be "baptized with the Holy Spirit" (Acts 1:5). Is it the same as being baptized in water? What are the benefits of the Spirit baptism? How can it be attained? How does it relate to spiritual manifestations, suffering, spiritual warfare, and the gift of tongues? Throughout this whole book, the Bible teaching will be illustrated by real-life experiences that confirm the Bible truth.

May you, dear reader, discover and enjoy more of God.

Chapter 1

The Word Alone Is Not Enough

The Holy Spirit Infilling

When I was growing up, I did not mind reading books, but my passion was sports. Every day we would kick the football around outdoors. At school I was not ambitious in getting good marks; but, at the same time, I was always curious about the meaning of life and seeking answers. From my earliest childhood, I had been a Christian; but confusion came in my teenage years because the truth of the Bible was contested even within the church. What was I to believe?

For some reason, I never doubted my call to be a pastor and was blessed when God took me out of Germany and placed me at Luther Seminary in Adelaide, Australia. I had found a place where Bible scholarship was combined with faith, and I began to immerse myself in the study of the Scriptures. More and more of my time would be spent in the library and, in later years, I was even trusted with my own key to the building. One of the tables was mine to use, and I would stack the table with piles of books.

At the seminary, the understanding was that an accurate interpretation of the Bible would yield the truth about everything—this was exciting! There were so many discoveries, but hidden beneath the surface there was also an omission in my learning. The Bible alone is not enough even though Lutherans, together with other Christian denominations, subscribe to the ancient slogan *sola scriptura* (Latin), which means in English that "the Word alone" is the sole source and authority over any teaching matter in the church. The slogan served a good purpose and is not in dispute; but at least in my personal understanding, there has nevertheless been an omission. I also needed something else.

When Jesus rose from the dead, He explained once again the purpose of His suffering and confronted the disciples with clear Bible teaching. In His own way, He confirmed the slogan of "the Word alone":

> *He said to them, "This is what I told you while I was still with you: Everything must be fulfilled that is written about me in the Law of Moses, the Prophets and the Psalms." Then he opened their minds so they could understand the Scriptures. He told them, "This is what is written: The Messiah will suffer and rise from the dead on the third day, and repentance for the forgiveness of sins will be preached in his name to all nations, beginning at Jerusalem"* (Luke 24:44-47 NIV; see also Luke 24:25-27).

Jesus opened the minds of the disciples to the Bible truths about His person so they would recognize that everything about Him was already foreshadowed and foretold in the Scriptures. They could trust "the Word alone," and on the basis of the Word preach sound sermons. They were in good shape when Jesus left them later on:

> *...he left them and was taken up into heaven...*[they] *returned to Jerusalem with* **great joy**. *And they stayed continually at the temple,* **praising God** (Luke 24:51-53).

After Jesus had instructed the disciples and left them praising God with joy, many of us would have considered them ready for action. When I finally graduated from our church seminary, I myself seemed ready for action because I also praised God, and there was enough learning in me to preach a solid exposition of the Scriptures. Therefore, with enthusiasm, I began to serve my first parish. The honeymoon period was great, and I may have looked like a young and promising pastor—but was I ready? I was not.

For all of my knowledge, plans, and programs, I presided over an aging and declining membership in an area that was younger than the national average. In six years, there was not a single convert.[1] No one blamed me for the lack of results, because my colleagues did not fare better and the denomination had become used to the decline. Yet, I became desperate and with good reason—for I was not ready.

When the first disciples had understood the Bible with much joy, Jesus cautioned them not to rush into preaching but wait in Jerusalem.

Something else was needed besides knowledge and praising God. The Word alone was not enough. This is what Jesus said to them:

> ...*Do not leave Jerusalem, but wait for the gift my Father promised, which you have heard me speak about. For John baptized with water, but in a few days you will be baptized with the Holy Spirit...you will receive power when the Holy Spirit comes on you; and you will be my witnesses in Jerusalem, and in all Judea and Samaria, and to the ends of the earth* (Acts 1:4-8; see also Luke 24:49).

It had never crossed my mind that I might need a greater measure of the Holy Spirit in my life. Pursuing knowledge and one theological degree after another, I valued "the Word alone" and assumed that "the Word alone" would get me across the line, irrespective of anything else. If the sermon was sound and true, it would not return empty. Yet, according to Acts 1, Jesus begged to differ and explained to His disciples that the Word of God alone was not enough but required the Spirit of God for power to unfold. Thus, the early church picked their ministers on the basis of Word competency and Spirit quantity:

> ...*choose seven men...who are known to be full of the Spirit and wisdom...* (Acts 6:3).

I was not used to this kind of thinking and it posed questions for me. How can you know that someone is full of the Spirit? Does the Spirit come with an experience and produce evidence that can be measured? Over the years, Lutherans like me have been quite uncomfortable with any personal reflection on Christian experience. This had not been part of my seminary training. I remember that in 2007 our congregation studied a resource with the title *Experiencing God: Knowing and Doing the Will of God*. One Sunday, an older and respected church member stood up in the worship service and said, "When we began the course, I felt like throwing the manual across the aisle. Don't you know, Pastor, that for us Lutherans the words 'experience' and 'obedience' are offensive?" He only expressed what we all felt. Around the same time, a colleague publicly thanked our president for allowing me to address Christian experience at the Lutheran Pastors' Conference. He had been waiting for this kind of debate for thirty years.

When I was a student at the church seminary, I did come to a point when I paused in my studies for reflection and began to wonder about the presence of the Spirit in my life but another one of the recommended books put my mind at rest. Its title was *The Holy Spirit: Shy Member of the Trinity*, and one of its core theses was that "those persons are most filled with the Spirit who are least conscious of it."[2] This quote put me at ease again because up to then I had not enjoyed any tangible experience of the Holy Spirit and, according to the book, this was okay. I was doing fine. In fact, my lack of experience had already placed me on a higher level of Spirit intensity in my life. Thus I felt free to go back to the library and fill my mind with knowledge, rather than the Spirit.

Confused by Baptism

There was another reason that blinded me to my need. I assumed that the fullness of the Spirit had been given to me in my water baptism. Lutherans have a high view of baptism in water, and any suggestion that there was another baptism in the Spirit would not be welcome because it would seem to undermine the gift of salvation, which is received in the first baptism (see 1 Pet. 3:21).

However, neither the Bible nor personal experience confirmed my traditional thinking. When another pastor baptized me with water, it was done, according to Jesus' command, "in the name of the Father and of the Son and of the Holy Spirit" (Matt. 28:19). I have no doubt that in this baptism I was born of the Spirit (see John 3:5), became a new creation (see 2 Cor. 5:17), was raised to live a new life (see Rom. 6:4), and became a child of God (Gal. 3:26-27). Thus established in my baptism; I grew up confessing my faith and I had the Spirit in me because "...no one can say, 'Jesus is Lord,' except by the Holy Spirit" (1 Cor. 12:3). I did not need more of the Spirit for salvation.

Yet, at closer examination, I realized that the experience of being baptized with the Spirit had nothing to do with salvation. It was a promise of power (see Luke 24:49; Acts 1:4-8). After Jesus had ascended to heaven, the disciples were praising God and enjoying their salvation. At that time, they were not lacking in faith but they were waiting for the baptism with the Spirit to make them powerful in mission. They only started preaching after it happened.

Therefore, the function of the water baptism and the further gift of the Spirit are not one and the same. The immersion in water gives us salvation; and the immersion in the Spirit grants us power. There is no competition between the two.

In the Bible, there seems to be a threefold process for every new believer, and it became the focus of attention early on because, after the disciples had preached their very first sermon, the people responded and asked them, "What shall we do?" (Acts 2:37). The disciples answered by encouraging the crowd to seize three distinct experiences that were available to everyone:

> **Repent** and **be baptized**, *every one of you, in the name of Jesus Christ for the forgiveness of your sins. And* **you will receive** *the gift of the Holy Spirit* (Acts 2:38).

The disciples asked the people 1) to repent, and 2) to be baptized (with water) for the forgiveness of their sins, so that 3) they would receive the gift of the Holy Spirit (meaning here the experience of being baptized with the Spirit). These three experiences were part of the process of becoming a believer and they all belonged together in the whole package of starting out as a Christian.

On the same day that someone repented, he or she could be baptized and receive the Spirit. Yet, there could also be time delays between repentance, baptism, and receiving the Spirit. For instance, in response to an encounter with Jesus, Saul repented but was not baptized before three days (see Acts 9:3-19). In the same way, it took some time for the new Christians in Samaria to receive the Spirit after their baptism:

> *When the apostles in Jerusalem heard that Samaria had accepted the word of God, they sent Peter and John to Samaria. When they arrived, they prayed for the new believers there that they might receive the Holy Spirit,* **because the Holy Spirit had not yet come on any of them; they had simply been baptized in the name of the Lord Jesus.** *Then Peter and John placed their hands on them, and they received the Holy Spirit* (Acts 8:14-17).

In the case of the Samaritans, the delay between baptism and receiving the Spirit was unusual; therefore it was immediately rectified—but confirms the basic distinction between water baptism and the gift of the Spirit in the process of becoming a Christian.

The threefold process of becoming a believer was not the same for everyone. In addition to time delays, people could experience the opposite. At one time, the Holy Spirit came on all who heard the preaching of Jesus before anyone could baptize them with water (see Acts 10:44-48). However, the more common sequence was the one laid out in the basic instruction of the disciples (Acts 2:38) and this is what was practiced:

> On hearing this, **they were baptized in the name of the Lord Jesus. When Paul placed his hands on them, the Holy Spirit came on them,** and they spoke in tongues and prophesied (Acts 19:5-6).

1) As people had turned to Jesus in repentance, 2) they were baptized first, and then 3) they received the Spirit. In this respect, Jesus' own baptism with water and the Spirit foreshadowed our experiences as we follow Him. He was also baptized with water first (John's baptism for the forgiveness of sins foreshadowing the later baptism in Jesus' name) and then was baptized with the Spirit. As other people repented and were baptized, Jesus Himself was also baptized, and when He emerged from the water, He was immediately immersed in the Holy Spirit as the Holy Spirit descended on him:

> When all the people were being baptized, **Jesus was baptized too. And as he was praying, heaven was opened and the Holy Spirit descended on him** in bodily form like a dove. And a voice came from heaven: "You are my Son, whom I love; with you I am well pleased" (Luke 3:21-22).

To this day, numerous people emerge from the water of their baptism with the same experience of being also immersed in the Holy Spirit. In fact, not disputing possible time delays, this is to be expected because these two experiences, with the experience of repentance, belong together at the beginning of the Christian life, but they are distinct from each other.[3]

For me as a Lutheran pastor, the whole Bible teaching on the threefold process of becoming a believer and receiving the Spirit after baptism with water proved challenging. It was not easy to read the Bible with fresh eyes and give up my traditional view. When I did, the church president paid me a visit and asked for an explanation. Together we looked at the Bible passages, and the evidence warranted only one conclusion. After repentance, a person would face two more experiences in water and the Spirit and, more to the point, this meant that baptism with water was not the same as receiving and being baptized with the Spirit; therefore, to add a further thought, there was no automatic guarantee that the baptized believer was also being baptized with the Spirit at the same time. In my own case, I knew that the two did not coincide. I was in my mid-thirties before I recognized my need for the Spirit and received Him.

Unknown Territory

I was on a steep learning curve. However, it is one thing to recognize that one's water baptism and God's Word alone are not enough, but it is another matter to start yearning for the Spirit. Where would I look for instruction and impartation? Would I have to go near the churches that we Lutherans considered "weird"? At this point, I may not have been immersed in the Spirit, but I was secure enough to know that I had the Spirit for salvation and my basic confession of faith because "…no one can say, 'Jesus is Lord,' except by the Holy Spirit" (1 Cor. 12:3). Therefore, would I want the risk of venturing into unknown territory? What would it cost me to upset familiar boundaries?

As it happened, my hunger and desperation for God were greater than any feelings of caution, and, to be precise, the Spirit came to me and our congregation not so much as the result of an active search but divine intervention. God took us by surprise.

In 2000, we began planting a less formal worship service in the chapel of Concordia College in Toowoomba, Australia. Within a year we had sufficient numbers to become a self-supporting congregation, and we loved our newfound freedom in using drama, modern music and bands, variations in the set worship order, and a more flexible preaching program. Our vision was to become a contemporary church like some other Lutheran churches across our nation. However, then God moved in and used our search for something fresh to impose His own vision.

In truth, He had been stirring us all along. Since 1996 the Lutheran youth of Toowoomba had been holding monthly Sunday night services with surprising results. Hundreds of young and older Christians would squeeze into the wooden pews to explore their faith with passion for something new. We wanted our faith to be real and, even early on, the youth kept asking me about the Spirit and spiritual gifts. They read the Bible, were mixing with a wider circle of friends, and were keen to explore everything that might be available.

I was not dragging my feet, but my formation in a traditional Lutheran mold was not always helping me. God needed to break my Lutheran pride and one early lesson was the retreat ministry of the Emmaus Walk. For three days, I was in an environment where the leadership and most other participants were not Lutherans, but they seemed to know something about God that was not yet in my own life. I had an experience of grace. The love of God became real for me like never before; this humbled me because I had come with the traditional Lutheran attitude of keeping my distance.

When I first arrived at the retreat camp, I was not quite certain whether the talks would measure up to my Lutheran standards, and I had my reservations about sharing the meal of Holy Communion with people who might not place the same high value on this meal as Lutherans. Yet over the three days of the retreat, God was dealing with me. There was something beyond my Lutheran standards that I had missed. Many people of the Emmaus Walk seemed to know more about faith and love than I did. God seemed to be more real to them than to me. This was humbling but was beginning to set me free and, over the next few years, many in our church had the same experience.

Then we discovered the Alpha Course; and in the first installment, more than fifty of our own members attended with the unexpected blessing of hearing basic teaching on the Holy Spirit for the first time in our lives. What we had intended for outreach became a source of our own faith renewal. We became more open and hungry in our attitudes.

God used still another strategy to stir us up for more. I had promised Pastor Colin Shaw from Toowoomba City Church that when I was no longer responsible for three Lutheran congregations and the combined Lutheran youth ministry in Toowoomba, I would join the local Christian Leaders' Network (CLN) and meet with them for weekly prayer. This is what I did. In 2002, our preaching place at Concordia College finally became the Living Grace Community Lutheran church; I was called as their pastor, and I began attending the prayer meetings of the Christian Leaders' Network, under the leadership of Pastor Ian Shelton from the Toowoomba City Church.

I took to the Christian Leaders' Network like a fish to water. My mind had been exercised about working together with others beyond the confines of congregational boundaries. Here, there were leaders who had a vision for an entire city and region. They worked with the assumption that there was only one church in the city of Toowoomba. In God, we belonged to each other and could work together in love. There was a kind of unity that had not been expressed in denominational structures but was based on trusting relationships.

Even though there were other mainline churches represented at CLN (for example, Anglican, Uniting Church, Presbyterian, Salvation Army, Wesleyan Methodist), I was the first Lutheran minister attending the prayer meetings, and I soon learned to appreciate a new culture. The practical importance of prayer was new. We would sit in a circle, sing a good number of songs, and pray together. At times, we would lay hands on some specific people and pray for their needs. I found that listening to my colleagues' prayers brought them closer to me than any theological debates.

I still remember the surprising response to my first contribution in 2003. We had planned to address some of the past conflicts between the churches and heal the hurts among so many of our members. At a public gathering in the Empire Theatre, we wanted to repent on behalf of our churches and ask those coming to the combined meeting for forgiveness. I decided to draft a paper on the theological understanding of this proposal. The paper was welcomed—but never discussed.

There was genuine appreciation for my work but no one saw the need to emulate the Lutheran culture and argue with each other until all possible differences of understanding were ironed out before we went ahead with our plans. This was new and fascinating. These pastors trusted each other enough to know that they had heard together from God. There was a unity of the Spirit that came before any perfect unity in understanding.

The CLN pastors had made prayer a priority, not theological debate, but their prayers and maturity taught me more than any lectures. God had put me in the right place. One Friday morning in 2002, we were again praying and singing in a circle. Most people were still standing and singing, but I was sitting down and praying. As I was saying the name of Jesus, all of a sudden I felt that some other words wanted to come out of my mouth. Before I knew it, I had opened my mouth and began to speak words that I did not understand. I asked myself, *What is this?* Then I concluded that this must be the gift of speaking in tongues. No special emotions came with this gift. No one else at the prayer meeting spoke in tongues, and no one noticed what had happened to me.

I was not particularly grateful for this gift because I had never wanted to speak words that I did not understand. Moreover, I knew that I could not go home and tell my wife. She had been praying to receive the gift of speaking in tongues for two years but to no avail, and now I had the gift against my own wishes. This would not have seemed fair to her. After a few weeks, I thought that I better share this experience with her. As I expected, she did struggle with God over this, and she had a point; but she was happy for me and, in time, began to speak in tongues herself.

What was I to do with this gift? I did not know. The obvious conclusion would have been that God wanted me to use this gift, but it took me months before I recognized the value of praying in tongues for my private devotions. Even then I used it sparingly and felt no need to promote speaking in tongues in our church. This was still unknown territory, and I knew that it would be stretching our Lutheran comfort zone. On the one hand, my excitement was growing but, on the other hand, this was beyond my understanding at the time. I needed to learn more about the Spirit.

Apart from me, God was also prodding and processing other members of our congregation. He was stirring us and increasing our hunger for a deeper relationship with Him. Then came His biggest surprise. A Lutheran pastor from Ethiopia was scheduled to tour our denomination in Australia. His name: Gemechis Desta Buba. I had not heard of him and knew nothing about the tour but received a phone call from the district church office asking me whether I would host him on January 1, 2003, because they had a vacant time slot for that Sunday.

We prepared for his visit, scheduling a Sunday night service and expecting a few worship songs and his preaching. About three hundred people came from across our region. Most of them were traditional

Lutherans. We sang about three songs before Pastor Gemechis began his sermon on the Lord's Prayer. It was a solid exposition, but when he came to the place where he declared that God was giving us our daily bread fresh each day, he stopped in the middle of his preaching and announced that he felt God prompting him to call us forward for prayer. This was not our usual practice.

However, to my surprise, most people in attendance that night made their way forward to receive prayer with the laying on of hands. I was even more surprised when about two-thirds of those receiving prayer proceeded to fall down under the power of the Holy Spirit. What was happening? I ended up trying to catch our church members as they were falling backward onto the floor, and I was thinking to myself, *What is this? Am I going to be in trouble with the church authorities?* Yet, that night no one objected to what was happening. Everyone sensed the presence of God in the worship building. I had never been in a service like that one.

There was no hype. The music was not loud, and Pastor Gemechis did not raise his voice or become emotional in other ways. Consequently, the prayer time was very accessible to traditional Lutherans. Yet, there was a new level of power. Some experienced the Spirit flooding their bodies with the peace of God. Others were simply wondering what pushed them to the floor. When Pastor Gemechis prayed for me, I made sure that my feet were solidly planted on the floor. God had permission to make me fall backward, but I would not be nimble on my feet. This would not have been the German way of my upbringing. As it happened, I stayed upright but was touched nevertheless. I received healing in my heart. All the hurt and rejection that came with planting a new church were washed away. This was an incredible gift and quite unexpected.

We had a memorable night. It was the night when God surprised our congregation with an experience that would take us years to understand in all of its dimensions—but it set us on our way. For the next five years we would debrief what had happened and how the Spirit might want to work among us. This would be a slow journey because I remember that, immediately after the service with Pastor Gemechis, two of our key leaders said, "We don't need to have this every Sunday." On the night I agreed, but later I began wondering, "Why would we not want more of this?"

The greater importance of this service only began to emerge slowly because God had a broader agenda than just teaching us on the Spirit. We had to learn so much more about prayer, forgiveness, inner healing, discipleship, church unity, and obedience. The night with Pastor Gemechis was only one seed among many that needed to grow among us. However, it was an important seed.

I discovered that the freedom of the night with Pastor Gemechis was not easily regained in normal church life. For years we were having difficulty in prayer ministry because our members were reluctant to leave the safety of the pews and come forward. This was not our traditional culture. We were also not used to being emotional or expressive in worship. It took me years before I felt comfortable enough to raise my hands in worship and reach out to God with greater passion. Even though I knew that this kind of worship was in the Bible and that Jesus Himself had raised His hands in worship, I felt bound by my church upbringing.

The phenomenon of falling down under the Spirit's power also caused tensions among us a long time after Pastor Gemechis had left. At first, there was no repeat of this manifestation for years. Then, I led a national Lutheran Prayer Summit in Adelaide in 2005 and had planned to close the three days of meetings with a communion service. By the time we were preparing for Holy Communion, I was absolutely exhausted. It was hard work to remain sensitive to the Spirit's leading and let Him set the prayer agenda in a group context. My last task was to pray for people with the laying on of hands as they were making their way to Holy Communion. I was so drained of all my energies that I felt sick and could not wait for the service to finish.

Then, a heavy-set man came up and stood before me. I prayed and had my eyes closed when I heard a mighty thud and realized that this man had crashed onto the hard wooden floor. I was shocked. My face expressed sheer horror, which provided significant amusement later on. I thought that this man had died of a heart attack on the way to Holy Communion. However, when I knelt next to him and saw that he was conscious, I asked him, "Are you all right?" He looked at me with uncomprehending eyes—he had received what he wanted. The Spirit of God was making him feel wonderful.

This was unexpected and new once again. Another woman also went down under prayer, but she caught herself and stayed upright. The sudden movement jarred her knee and she said, "This was not comfortable." I apologized to her, but what could I do? Still another woman stood in front of me and asked for prayer. She explained that she had been running away from God and wanted to stop running. I prayed, and she also fell to the floor; she lay there with a contorted face. What was going on with her? I knelt next to her and asked if she was all right. She said, "I'm fine." However, she did not look fine to me and, without thinking, I laid hands on her again and said, "Whatever makes you run, leave now." Immediately, her face turned to one side, completely relaxed, and she seemed to be sound asleep like a baby. What was that? Did I just drive out a demon? This was quite a remarkable finish to our Prayer Summit; I learned something about the power that comes from sustained prayer and how God is not dependent on my feelings. My exhaustion did not stop Him.

It would take almost another two years before another person would fall under the power of the Spirit in our church. For me this seemed to be a long time, but for others this manifestation remained controversial. Five years after Pastor Gemechis' visit, our congregation agreed on the teaching of the Holy Spirit. We accepted the testimonies from other people and places, but more visible displays of power in our own Sunday morning services and prayer ministry were another matter. Then, more and more people received the gift of tongues and this also raised the level of discomfort among some of our members. In time, there was a parting of ways and a number of the members broke away in an amicable manner.

When I was first reflecting on Pastor Gemechis' visit, I discovered that I had been misreading First Corinthians 2:1-5, which is a favorite Bible passage for Lutherans:

> *…For I resolved to know nothing while I was with you except Jesus Christ and him crucified. I came to you in weakness with great fear and trembling. My message and my preaching were not with wise and persuasive words, **but with a demonstration of the Spirit's power**, so that your faith might not rest on human wisdom, but on God's power* (1 Corinthians 2:1-5).

I was stunned. How could I get this familiar Bible passage so wrong? We Lutherans agree with the initial thrust of the reading. The central message of the Christian faith is "Jesus Christ and him crucified," and we make the further correct observation that the cross of Jesus is hiding God's power. God, in general, seems to work with the principle of being powerful in apparent weakness (see 1 Cor. 1:25-31). This worked on the cross as Jesus died but saved the world, and this seems to work in our preaching as we speak "foolish" words about a crucified Savior (see 1 Cor. 1:18) but offer eternal life. There is encouragement in our weakness because this seems to be God's way of working salvation.

This had been my Lutheran understanding, but it was incomplete as far as First Corinthians 2:1-5 is concerned. The preaching may be "in weakness," and there may not be any "wise and persuasive words," but God purposed to back up the message of Jesus and Him crucified "with a demonstration of the Spirit's power." Faith would not come through preaching alone but would rest on a demonstration of "God's power"—this is what happened on the night that Pastor Gemechis ministered to us in Toowoomba.

On further investigation, the apostle Paul summed up his entire ministry by explaining that preaching and demonstrations of power belonged together:

> *I will not venture to speak of anything except what Christ has accomplished through me in leading the Gentiles to obey God by what I have said and done—**by the power of signs and wonders, through the power of the Spirit of God**. So from Jerusalem all the way around to Illyricum, I have fully proclaimed the gospel of Christ* (Romans 15:18-19).

Over the years, I became more and more desperate to do ministry and mission work in the same way. My understanding had been that persuasive preaching would prove attractive to searching people and garner converts, but how would I make the virgin birth and the divine nature of Jesus plausible to the modern mind? Jesus and the disciples had their preaching always confirmed with healings, confrontations with demons, signs and wonders. I wanted the same in our church.

Year after year in report after report, I would express this goal for our church. Then, in 2009 we came to the last Sunday of the year and we were all in need of rest. The past twelve months had been packed with new developments, not least the purchase of our first worship home. We needed an uplifting service; therefore, I decided to preach on the glory of God. I enjoyed dwelling on the glory of God that shone around the shepherds on the night of Jesus' birth.

At some point in the sermon, I announced that God's glory had come to our Living Grace congregation, and then I provided some evidence. Three months earlier, I had been preaching a series on healing for six consecutive nights at another Toowoomba church. At the conclusion of one service, we discovered that two of our older members had gold flakes on their faces. What was that? We never had that before. It was a manifestation that came out of the glory presence of God. I had only become aware of such miracles two years previous.

Then I shared that at our regular prayer meeting on a Friday night, six weeks earlier, we saw a kind of mist under the ceiling. It was as if there was a small smoke machine in the church. I thought that it must have come from the outside. Everyone could see the mist, but others assured me that it had not come in through the window. It was the glory cloud of God that stayed for about one and a half hours. Previously, we only knew the Bible accounts of this phenomenon and testimonies from church history, but now it was in our own church.

Finally, two weeks before the sermon I was praying for a woman who ended up on the floor weeping and repenting to God. Suddenly I could see something sparkling on her. The black skin on the back of her hand was covered with fine gold glitter. I turned her hand but there was nothing on her palms. Two minutes later I checked again and now her palms were also covered in fine gold glitter. I tapped her on the shoulder and said, "Stop crying. Look, what God is doing for you. He loves you. He makes you look beautiful. You are His princess."

I kept preaching about the glory of God at Living Grace on the last Sunday of 2009; and at the conclusion of the service, invited the entire congregation to check their hands to see if they had received gold dust as well. This was not planned; and everyone who checked their hands that morning had the miracle. I rejoiced in God—and ever since, the gold dust has been manifesting at Living Grace. For two and a half years now, members and visitors receive the glory sparkles in our church. As people share the testimony of the miracle, it may appear on them and those who hear the testimony. This also happens during the week. People are coming to faith through the miracle because it confounds the rational mindset and confirms the preaching of Jesus. Numerous times, I have prayed for other congregations to receive the miracle and it manifested among the people. This has been wonderful for us. The glory of God has come into our midst. Our youngest daughter, Francisca, seems to have the gold sparkles all of the time.

However, I also discovered that this was another work of the Spirit that was not welcome among all Christians. For weeks and months our own members were debating the miracle. At the height of the confusion, some thought that it was the devil that was making the gold sparkles appear. The temptation, then, was to downplay the miracle and ignore the manifestation; but this would have been ungrateful and would have contradicted our express desire to see the preaching confirmed with a "demonstration of the Spirit's power."

When I shared our experiences with other local pastors, I was met with indifference and a lack of enthusiasm. No one was hostile, but apart from some exceptions, there was not much joy either. This led to another new experience. Four weeks later, I shed a few tears in church. I was grieving over our rejection of God and His goodness toward us. As I was preaching, I felt as if God was sharing His own emotions with me and He seemed to be grieving over our reluctance to embrace His glory presence. We came through this season and now the whole church and many other pastors and congregations are sharing the joy over God's tangible touches of love. The determined resolve to rejoice in miracles broke through the barriers of fear. Who knows what other miracles God may provide for us? There have already been manifestations of oil appearing on people's hands, so therefore we keep celebrating the birth of new Christians, healings, deliverance from demons, love, and supernatural joy.

For now, this may be enough of our journey. From what I have shared, you can conclude that it has not always been easy to embrace the Spirit. Not only was I confronted with the new understanding that the Word alone, without the Spirit, was not enough and that my baptism in water was not the same as receiving the Spirit, I was at risk of encountering unknown territory where the Spirit would do new things outside of my control. There was a price to pay.

ENDNOTES

1. There may have been one or two who happened to fall in love with a Lutheran girl.

2. F. Dale Bruner, "The Shy Member of the Trinity—Expository Preaching Gives the Filling of the Holy Spirit," 11-33, in Frederick Dale Bruner and William Hordern, eds: *The Holy Spirit, Shy Member of the Trinity* (Minneapolis, MN: Augsburg Publishing House, 1984), 13. (My past understanding of the book does not adequately reflect its content and more balanced insights.)

3. Consider also Ephesians 1:13.

Chapter 2

The Bible Describes the Spirit Baptism

Surprisingly, the Bible nowhere gives a definition of the baptism with the Spirit. However, from the beginning, Jesus' own work was defined as baptizing people. This was what would be new with the coming of Jesus and, at least to John the Baptist, this seemed to matter the most:

> *The beginning of the good news about Jesus the Messiah, the Son of God. ...And so John the Baptist appeared in the wilderness, preaching a baptism of repentance for the forgiveness of sins. ... And this was his message: "After me comes the one more powerful than I, the straps of whose sandals I am not worthy to stoop down and untie. **I baptize you with water, but he will baptize you with the Holy Spirit** (Mark 1:1-8).*

John the Baptist was the forerunner of Jesus. He offered forgiveness but not the power of the Spirit. Therefore, he was inferior to Jesus. He was not worthy even to untie Jesus' sandals because Jesus would not only baptize people with water but the Holy Spirit. This meant that, in addition to forgiveness through water, there would be power for holy living and the kingdom of God would be near.

Jesus Himself acknowledged the value of being baptized in the Spirit with radical words:

> *But very truly I tell you, it is for your good that I am going away. Unless I go away, the Advocate will not come to you; but if I go, I will send him to you* (John 16:7).

What could be better than having Jesus lead the disciples and provide for them? Jesus was preaching with authority, healing the sick, raising the dead, driving out demons, and, on occasion, multiplying food. Therefore, what could be more advantageous for the disciples than Jesus as their companion? Jesus pointed to the Spirit. If He left them, the Holy Spirit would be sent and come to them. This would be truly for their good because the Spirit was worth that much.

Only, how would people receive Him? How would the Holy Spirit come on people? The earlier words of John the Baptist give us an important clue. He said, "I baptize you with water, but he will baptize you with the Holy Spirit." The experience of receiving the Spirit would resemble the baptism with water whereby the whole body of a person was being submerged and washed in water. Jesus would practice the same mode of baptism except that the whole person would be submerged and washed in the Spirit. As John immersed and soaked a person in water, so Jesus would immerse and soak a person in the Spirit.

Therefore, what people may expect is a stronger experience of the Spirit. John neither defined nor explained what Jesus would do precisely, but the image of baptism and being submerged in the Spirit suggest something of an overwhelming nature. Jesus would not just release drops of the Spirit but plunge us into His abundance, and this would be reflected in the experience. This does not mean that everyone must expect dramatic manifestations, but that everyone receives much and is impacted for good.

The Bible descriptions of people being baptized with the Spirit bear this out:

> *Suddenly **a sound like the blowing of a violent wind** came from heaven and filled the whole house where they were sitting. They saw what seemed to be **tongues of fire** that separated and came to rest on each of them. All of them were filled with the Holy Spirit and began to **speak in other tongues** as the Spirit enabled them. …When they heard this sound, a crowd came together in bewilderment, because each one heard their own language being spoken. …Amazed and perplexed, they asked one another, "What does this mean?" Some, however, made fun of them and said, "**They have had too much wine**"* (Acts 2:2-13).

Peter explained:

Exalted to the right hand of God, [Jesus] *has received from the Father the promised Holy Spirit and has poured out **what you now see and hear*** (Acts 2:33).

*...the Holy Spirit came on all who heard the message. The circumcised believers who had come with Peter were astonished that the gift of the Holy Spirit had been poured out even on Gentiles. For they heard them **speaking in tongues and praising God*** (Acts 10:44-46).

*When Paul placed his hands on them, the Holy Spirit came on them, and they **spoke in tongues and prophesied*** (Acts 19:6).

In every instance, the people who were being baptized with the Spirit knew that they had an experience, and bystanders also recognized that something was happening. On occasion, a crowd gathered. People could "see and hear" phenomena that were caused by the Spirit. Yet the experience was not always the same. Only once is there a report of a sound like the blowing of a violent wind and what seemed to be tongues of fire engulfing the disciples. More common was the sudden release of spiritual gifts such as speaking in tongues and prophecy. People would be joyful and praise God.

The same observation can be made today as Jesus keeps baptizing people with the Spirit. Not everyone has the same experience. Some simply feel their hearts strangely warmed. Others have strong bodily reactions. They may begin to shake or fall down like struck by lightning. It does not matter what manifestations the Spirit causes. The experiences may vary, but the same Spirit comes in fullness to everyone.

When the Spirit came on the disciples for the first time, there were some in the crowd who accused them of drunkenness, saying, "They have had too much wine." What gave rise to the accusation? The disciples must have looked unsteady on their feet or maybe their speech was slurred. Interestingly, the Spirit still has the same effect on people today. There are some who, under the influence of the Spirit, look drunk. This had never happened to me; but observing this phenomenon in others, it looked like a happy experience.

Then in 2010, God spoke to me about abstaining from alcohol. This was not what I wanted to hear. Lutherans enjoy their glass of red wine and both my grandparents had owned vineyards. At first I listened, but abstained from alcohol only for a season because I did not hear God say, "Never have alcohol again."

However, He spoke to me again about drinking no alcohol. I asked Him, "Why? I don't have a problem with alcohol, and I enjoy relaxing in this way." He answered, "I want you to be on constant alert." The spiritual warfare would not cease. I struggled with this new directive. After all, Jesus Himself had turned water into wine. I put this question to God, "What will I get in return?" This was bold, but I felt like He was willing to strike a deal with me. I was allowed to ask for something.

Right away, the Bible passage of Ephesians 1:18 came to my mind where the admonishment was not to be drunk on wine but the Holy Spirit. I said to God, "As you take alcohol away from me, please make me drunk in the Spirit." I printed out the sentence, "You will be DRUNK in the SPIRIT" and posted it next to my computer screen. This was God's promise to me. He would be faithful—and He was. Only He kept His promise with a sense of humor. The first time I was drunk in the Spirit happened while I was preaching (September 2010). As I was concentrating on the words, God enjoyed making me look unsteady on my feet and slowing down my delivery. In the end, I needed a chair and a short rest before I could continue.

This kind of manifestation does not happen to everyone, but everyone experiences the Spirit and being baptized with the Spirit in some way. Most importantly, when the Spirit comes, He is bearing fruit in a person's life, and the Bible identifies some of the fruit as being love, joy, and peace (see Gal. 5:22-23). This kind of fruit always comes with an emotional experience.

Person or Substance

When John announced that he baptized with water but Jesus would baptize with the Spirit, he drew a parallel between water and the Spirit. As people could be immersed in the substance of water, so they could be immersed in the Spirit. Apparently, there is something about the

Spirit that has the quality of abundant water because Jesus Himself mentioned this in further references. Jesus said:

*"Whoever believes in me, as Scripture has said, **rivers of living water will flow from within them.**" By this he meant the Spirit, whom those who believed in him were later to receive. Up to that time the Spirit had not been given, since Jesus had not yet been glorified* (John 7:38-39).

*But whoever drinks the water I give them will **never thirst**. Indeed, the water I give them will become in them a **spring of water welling up to eternal life*** (John 4:14).

According to these verses, the Spirit of God may be experienced like water but, in other places, the Bible also suggests that the Spirit may resemble or cause the same effect as fire (see Matt. 3:11; Acts 2:3), wind or breath (see Acts 2:2; John 3:8; Ezek. 37:9-10), oil (see Luke 4:18; Acts 10:38; 1 John 2:20,27; Ps. 23:5), and clothing (see Luke 24:49; Judges 6:34; 2 Kings 2:13-14). Thus, in summary, the Bible is using language for the Spirit that explains that the Spirit is often experienced like a substance or nature phenomenon.

Accordingly, the receiving of the Spirit is frequently compared to the receiving of a substance. The Bible can speak of the Spirit as being poured out on people or being smeared on people. People are said to be filled with the Spirit. Thus, the Spirit seems to behave like some sort of fluid that is released in larger measures:

*In the last days, God says, I will **pour out my Spirit** on all people. ...I will **pour out my Spirit** in those days, and they will prophesy* (Acts 2:17-18; see also Acts 2:33; 10:45).

*All of them were **filled with the Holy Spirit**...* (Acts 2:4; see also Acts 4:8,31; 6:3,5; 7:55; 9:17; 11:24; 13:9,52).

The challenge of this kind of language is a possible misunderstanding. The Holy Spirit may have some of the same qualities as water, fire, and oil, but He is a person, not a substance. What we are to understand in all of the imagery is that the baptism with the Spirit grants us unlimited access to the person of the Holy Spirit. There is full intimacy that may feel like an immersion into a substance, but it is His holy presence. We are His temple where He resides permanently (see 1 Cor. 6:19).

The Holy Spirit is a person. In fact, in the mystery of our one God, He is the third person, next to the Father and the Son; and, thus, every believer is to be baptized "in the name of the Father, and of the Son, *and of the Holy Spirit*" (Matt. 28:19). Jesus also called Him the Advocate and the Spirit of truth:

> *...**the Advocate**...I will send him to you. When he comes, he will prove the world to be in the wrong about sin and righteousness and judgment...But when **he, the Spirit of truth**, comes, he will guide you into all the truth. ...He will glorify me...* (John 16:7-14).

Thus in our experiences with Him, we learn to relate to the Spirit as a person, not a substance. The Spirit has a mind (see Rom. 8:27; 1 Cor. 2:10-13), will (see 1 Cor. 12:11), and emotions (see Rom. 8:26-27; 15:30; Col. 1:8). Lying to Him is lying to God (see Acts 5:3-4). What the Spirit wants is that we fellowship with Him (see 2 Cor. 13:14) and be sensitive to Him as He draws us into the worship of the Father through the Son. Together with Him, we await the return of Jesus and say to the Son of God, "Come!" (Rev. 22:17).

In my own practice, I am still discovering how this is meant to work. Instead of having a fixed prayer agenda, I like to spend some time inquiring whether my attention should be focused on the Father or the Son or the Holy Spirit. It is not always the same. Sometimes I am drawing near to "our Father" (Matt. 6:9) with the Spirit impressing on me that I am a son of God (see Rom. 8:15); and then, by Him, I cry out, "Abba, Father" (see Gal. 4:6). At other times, Jesus is dearest to me, and I begin my prayers with, "Lord Jesus" (Acts 7:59). I know that this happens again by the Spirit who is always bringing glory to Him (see John 16:14).

Frequently in these prayer times, I sense the overwhelming presence of the Spirit, but I am still slow to recognize Him as a person. In the Bible, there seem to be no instances where people pray to the Holy Spirit (see John 15:26), but I want to worship and respect Him. If my body is His temple, I want to be His friend. He is not a substance or commodity—He is a person.

Three Main Benefits

For a long time I was confused about the precise role of the Spirit in my life. Everyone seemed to focus on a different aspect of His work but not spell out the bigger picture. What made it difficult to bring order into my thinking was the fact that the Holy Spirit permeates absolutely everything in the church and the individual believer. Without Him, nothing happens in the Christian life because we "live by the Spirit" (Gal. 5:25). Whatever we know about God, He revealed to us. Whatever we have accomplished, He made happen by His power.

Yet, in time, I came to identify three main benefits that come from being baptized with the Spirit. Jesus promised that we "will receive power when the Holy Spirit comes" (Acts 1:8) on us, and this power, then, serves three basic outcomes: 1) The Spirit assures us of salvation; 2) The Spirit grants us victory over sin and empowers us to holiness; and 3) The Spirit expands the kingdom of God and makes us successful in mission work. Thus, the three main benefits of our immersion in the Spirit are in three words: 1) assurance, 2) holiness, and 3) mission.

It is further helpful to see the baptism with the Spirit as the pivotal experience in the Christian life because from this vantage point we can look both backward and forward. We look backward to our conversion and receive the assurance that we are being saved. By the Spirit, all doubts are being removed. Then, we look forward to our maturing life as Christians and, through the Spirit, receive power for the ongoing work of personal holiness and reaching out to others in mission work. These three main benefits are crucial for every believer, and I will spend some time expanding on them.

A few years back, one of my Lutheran colleagues, a retired pastor, shocked me because he shared with me how another dying Christian was plagued by doubts and uncertainties. Then he said, "You know, in my long experience as a minister, this happens often when our Lutheran church members are close to death. The struggle with one's conscience continues right to the drawing of one's last breath."

I could not accept this reality. Should this really be the standard experience of dying Christians? Are we all meant to die in fear and uncertainty? I know that we can all be tempted and I accept that the deathbed can be another fierce battleground. However, there are Bible accounts where dying Christians have been seeing "the glory of God, and Jesus standing at the right hand of God" (Acts 7:55); and there are modern testimonies of equal faith assurances right to the end of one's life.

One day, I was prayer-walking near our home, and as I was walking up a hill, I thought I heard a faint cry. I looked into the front yard of the next house, and there was an elderly woman lying on the footpath. The sun was beating down on her, but she was unable to move, unable to crawl into the shade. As I approached, she looked up at me and said, "Thank you, God, for sending me one of your own." She was a Christian and had prayed for help; when I came, she recognized me from a video. I helped her into the house. She shared with me that she had just returned from the hospital. In the course of the conversation, she also shared how she always expected at least one convert each time she had to stay in the hospital. She went to the hospital for mission work.

Some time later she died, and according to her daughter, this is what transpired. A few years back, the woman had four bypass surgeries, and God seemed to tell her then that if she wanted, she could go home to heaven; but she replied to Him that she did not want to go home before her work on earth was finished. So she lived on. Then, the year before her death, a cancer was growing behind her nose and this affected one eye. It was closing permanently and lumps appeared under her chin. By this time, she was eighty-eight years old, could no longer cope with the anaesthetic, had another heart attack, and simply stayed at the hospice.

She was a person filled with the Holy Spirit, but some days before she died, under the influence of various drugs, she was being attacked by doubts. Her daughter sensed this and asked her, "Do you know that you are being saved?" Then the daughter felt led to make this 100 percent certain and lead her mother one more time through the sinner's prayer. She prayed something like this, "Lord Jesus Christ, I am sorry for the things that I have done wrong in my life. Please forgive me. Thank You, Lord Jesus. Amen."

After the daughter had led her mother through this prayer, peace came over the mother and she was smiling with the most beautiful smile. About three days before she died, the family sensed that Jesus had come into the room and was now sitting on her bed. He was waiting for her to come with Him to heaven. On the last evening, she could no longer talk but she looked at her daughter, and the daughter understood the look. She asked her mother, "Is it time to go now?" The woman answered with the most beautiful smile. So the daughter prayed and asked Jesus to take her mother home. Then, in a moment, the mother was no longer looking at the daughter but at a spot above her. Her smiling face was incredible. She was seeing Jesus; and when she was seeing Jesus, according to her daughter, she was being healed. Her eye opened and she was again seeing with both eyes. The lumps under her chin disappeared, and then finally, her heart stopped. She went home with a healed body and so much joy.

Assurance is promised to all of us. We do not have to live and die in fear and misery but can know that we belong to God and that heaven is waiting for us. When Jesus Himself was being baptized with the Spirit, He was being assured of His identity in God. As the Spirit descended on Him, immediately he heard the voice of the Father from heaven saying to Him, "You are my Son, whom I love; with you I am well pleased" (Mark 1:11). This is what happens in anyone's baptism with the Spirit. We receive the Holy Spirit who is bearing witness with us that we are the children of God. By Him, we trust that God is our Father whom we call "Abba." There is assurance:

> ...*the Spirit you received brought about your adoption to sonship. And by him we cry, "**Abba**, Father." The Spirit himself testifies with our spirit that we are God's children* (Romans 8:15-16; see also Galatians 4:6; 1 John 3:24).

In other places, the Bible identifies the gift of assurance as the seal of the Holy Spirit or the deposit of the Holy Spirit, which is the experienced guarantee of our eternal inheritance:

> ...*He anointed us, set his seal of ownership on us, and put his Spirit in our hearts as a deposit, guaranteeing what is to come* (2 Corinthians 1:21-22).

> ...*God, who has given us the Spirit as a deposit, guaranteeing what is to come* (2 Corinthians 5:5).

> ...*When you believed, you were marked in him with a seal, the promised Holy Spirit, who is a deposit guaranteeing our inheritance...* (Ephesians 1:13-14).

There are still plenty of occasions where "we live by faith, not by sight" (2 Cor. 5:7), but basic assurance is ours. We are the children of God, and we know our future in Him. I may add that the Spirit's work of assurance is of special interest to Lutherans like me because it confirms the breakthrough of understanding that God had entrusted to Martin Luther. We are being justified by faith, not works. Salvation is a gift of grace, not merit. When the immersion in the Spirit comes, this core truth becomes alive to us so that our faith "is confidence in what we hope for and assurance about what we do not see" (Heb. 11:1).[1]

The gift of assurance is a wonderful experience, but the baptism with the Holy Spirit is promising us even more. John the Baptist came before Jesus and prepared the way for Him. John preached a baptism of repentance for the forgiveness of sins. Then, he baptized people with water, but he knew that he was lacking in power. In response to his preaching, people could repent and be forgiven, but they would not receive the necessary power for lasting changes. Sin could not be conquered permanently by a baptism with water. Thus, John declared:

> *...After me comes the one more powerful than I, the straps of whose sandals I am not worthy to stoop down and untie. I baptize you with water, but he will baptize you with the Holy Spirit* (Mark 1:7-8).

The good news was that Jesus, through the baptism with the Spirit, would empower the repentance of people and make them victorious over temptations and sin. The Holy Spirit would work holiness in them and this was Jesus' own experience first. When He was being baptized with the Spirit, Jesus received the strength to endure severe temptations and an immediate forty-day battle experience with satan in the wilderness. The Bible records that "full of the Holy Spirit" Jesus was being "led by the Spirit" into the desert to be "tempted by the devil" (Luke 4:1-2). Without the Spirit, Jesus would have failed, but "full of the Holy Spirit," He prevailed in holiness. It is the same for us.

We seek the baptism with the Spirit so that sin shall not be our master. By the Spirit, we conquer any temptations:

> *For sin shall no longer be your master...* (Romans 6:14).

> *...by the Spirit you put to death the misdeeds of the body...* (Romans 8:13).

...live by the Spirit, and you will not gratify the desires of the sinful nature (Galatians 5:16 NIV 1984).

Finally, the goal of the baptism with the Spirit is to make us ready for mission work. This outcome was also experienced by Jesus first. His Spirit baptism prepared Him for His work so that He declared:

> *The Spirit of the Lord is on me, because he has anointed me to preach good news to the poor. He has sent me to proclaim freedom for the prisoners and recovery of sight for the blind, to set the oppressed free, to proclaim the year of the Lord's favor* (Luke 4:18-19).

In the same way as Jesus, we need to have the Spirit on us and be anointed by Him so that we also have the power to preach the good news to the poor and proclaim freedom to the oppressed. This was Jesus' declared objective for His disciples when He told them to stay in Jerusalem and wait for the baptism with the Spirit. At the time of the Spirit's coming upon them, they would receive power to be His witnesses. Jesus said to them:

> *...wait for the gift my Father promised...in a few days you will be baptized with the Holy Spirit. ...But you will receive power when the Holy Spirit comes on you; and you will be my witnesses in Jerusalem, and in all Judea and Samaria, and to the ends of the earth* (Acts 1:4-8).

For years, trusting Jesus' promise, I had prayed that the Spirit's power for mission would also become a greater reality in our church. Then, in the spring of 2006,[2] I thought I heard God say to me on a Sunday morning, "During the service, I want you to give an altar call for salvation." I thought, *Okay*. However, the first service was not well-attended, and I was shivering in the early morning cold. There were about twenty-five people, and I thought I knew them all. Thus, after the message, I decided that I would wait to give the altar call until after our second service, which was the main worship time for Living Grace.

I sat down after the preaching in the first service, but immediately a man stood up from one of the back pews. His name was David Challenor, and he had never been to Living Grace before. Somehow I had not seen him even though he was of considerable size and his arms were covered with tattoos. He said, "I have a fourteen-year-old boy with me and he wants to come to the Lord. Can anyone help him?" I felt the gentle rebuke of God and prayed, "I'm sorry. I will be more obedient next time and trust You." We stopped what we were doing and invited the pair to the front. I led the teenager in a prayer, and we were all rejoicing in his salvation.

There was more rejoicing when we found out how God had blessed David so that the teenage boy ended up in his care. A few years back, David had been a drug addict, a violent member of a motorbike gang, and a convicted criminal who had spent time in prison. Yet God had called him to a new life in Christ and allowed him to give something back to the community. Even the police began to trust him to the extent that they, on their own accord, had contacted him and had asked for his help to provide shelter to the fourteen-year-old boy. David took him into his home and then to church. At first he thought that he was in the wrong congregation, but God knew better. The teenager found salvation; and in time, David became the full-time evangelist of the Living Grace community.

This is only one testimony of how the Spirit empowers us for mission. He speaks to us and sets up appointments. He moves on people's hearts and makes sure that the Word of God does not return empty.

I repeat the three main benefits that come from being baptized with the Spirit. We receive: 1) assurance, 2) victory over sin, and 3) power for mission work. All of these benefits came to Jesus first as He was being baptized with the Spirit. He received assurance when a voice came to Him from heaven, saying, "You are my Son, whom I love" (Mark 1:11). He received victory over sin when the Spirit empowered Him to withstand the temptations immediately following His baptism, and He received power for mission that enabled him to preach with authority, heal the sick, and drive out demons.

For all believers, the baptism with the Spirit is the pivotal experience in the Christian life. It enables us to look backward to our conversion with assurance and look forward with confidence to the ongoing work of personal holiness and reaching out to others in mission work. What is common to all of these benefits is that we "receive power when the Holy Spirit comes" (Acts 1:8).

ENDNOTES

1. Emil Wacker, *Ordo Salutis* (Breklum: Christian Jensen Verlag, 1960) 5.

2. November 19, 2006.

Chapter 3

Receiving the Holy Spirit Is for Everyone

When Jesus rose from the dead, He met up again with His disciples and, as the risen Lord, impressed on them the message of salvation. He summed up the meaning of what they had experienced with Him before saying:

> *This is what is written: The Messiah will suffer and rise from the dead on the third day, and repentance for the forgiveness of sins will be preached in his name to all nations, beginning at Jerusalem. You are witnesses of these things* (Luke 24:46-48).

With these words, Jesus explained again His person to the disciples and established Himself as the content of the salvation message. It was all about Him. On account of Him and in His name, the disciples would preach repentance and forgiveness to all nations.

Later, Jesus would expand on His plans and draw their attention to the Holy Spirit. He would tell them not to leave Jerusalem until they had been immersed in the Spirit; but by then, the focus was firmly set on His person. Salvation would be in no other name but Jesus; therefore, the coming Spirit would not detract from any devotion to Jesus but serve the purpose of bringing glory to Him, as Jesus Himself declared, "…the Spirit…will not speak on his own…He will glorify me…" (John 16:13-14).

Before Jesus prepared the stage for the Holy Spirit, He made clear that He would remain the focus of the disciples' work. Salvation would be in His name. The Spirit would not draw attention to His own person but rather empower the preaching of Jesus. This may be important to remember as this chapter is about the excitement of receiving the Holy Spirit.

Two Preliminary Remarks

A few years back someone explained to me why Germans seem to find it so hard to receive and enjoy the Holy Spirit. According to this person, Germans are too analytical and technical. They get a taste of the Spirit; then tend to write precise manuals on His operation while the Spirit is not quite as rigid in His movements. I am of German background, and I have come to appreciate this viewpoint.

After ten years of absence from my homeland, I returned for a visit and was astounded by what I was reading in a women's magazine. There was an ad for a plastic thong (sandal) which listed seven scientific reasons why this plastic thong was of superior engineering quality than its competitors. A cheap plastic thong is not a high-tech device but, apparently, German women had no problem accepting that precise engineering was the top attraction for even their most basic footwear. Where else do people behave like Germans? Engineering excellence is part of their culture and makes them high achievers, but the scientific mindset also causes them problems with the Spirit of God because there is not one precise method for receiving the Spirit and commanding His presence.

There is no manual and no control of God. No engineering prowess can get hold of Him because He remains sovereign and creative. For instance, only in Acts 2 was there a "sound like the blowing of a violent wind" (Acts 2:2) and what "seemed to be tongues of fire" (Acts 2:3). According to one report, the Holy Spirit came on the people of Samaria after they had been baptized in water and the apostles placed their hands on them (see Acts 8:16-17). However, in another report, the Holy Spirit came upon an entire family before they were baptized in water and before anyone could place their hands on them. They received the Spirit as they listened to the preaching of the good news through Jesus Christ (see Acts 10:44-48). At one time, the Spirit caused the speaking in tongues and praise (see Acts 10:46), and at another time, His coming caused the speaking in tongues and prophecy (see Acts 19:6).

There is no manual that can prescribe with precision how people receive the Holy Spirit. There are no fixed procedures and scientific certainties—even for Germans. All we have are principles that prepare us to receive the Holy Spirit in the way that God has intended for us. Thus, this chapter is dealing with principles, not unbendable laws. God, with loving care, will tailor the experience of being baptized with the Spirit for every person according to his or her needs.

In addition to this observation, we need to add another preliminary remark. When Jesus promised the disciples that they would receive the Holy Spirit, He was not suggesting that they would receive the Holy Spirit only once and then control Him as their certain possession. There is no static arrangement for any Christian; but our relationship with the Spirit is, from beginning to end, dynamic in character. Thus, the same principles for receiving the Spirit are the principles we keep applying in the Christian life, because after the first coming of the Spirit there needs to be further top-up experiences.

After their first immersion in the Spirit, the disciples soon realized that this experience of immersion needed to happen again because no person remains in a state of being completely saturated in the Spirit. The intensity of the Spirit wanes; therefore, there is always a fresh need of being saturated or filled with the Spirit. For this reason, the Bible encourages us to keep being "filled with the Spirit" (Eph. 5:18). We have a need to keep applying the principles that allow Him to come in fullness.

Let us unpack this further. After His resurrection, Jesus taught the disciples about Himself and thus established them as people of faith who "worshiped him" and "stayed continually at the temple, praising God" (Luke 24:52-53). At this time, they were not yet baptized with the Holy Spirit, but the Holy Spirit was nevertheless at work in the disciples because, according to the Bible, "…no one can say, 'Jesus is Lord,' except by the Holy Spirit" (1 Cor. 12:3).[1] They were in the same position as other Christians who have begun to trust and worship Jesus but have not yet received the full immersion in the Spirit.

For the disciples, the baptism with the Spirit happened on the day of Pentecost (see Acts 2), and they received the Holy Spirit with a "sound like the blowing of a violent wind" and what "seemed to be tongues of fire" (Acts 2:2-3). There was preaching with power and about three thousand converts.

Yet, only a few days later, there was a fresh need of encouragement and a fresh need to receive the very same Holy Spirit with all of His power. In the face of persecution, the disheartened disciples came together for prayer, and at the end of the prayer, the Bible records:

> ...*The place where they were meeting was shaken. And **they were all filled with the Holy Spirit** and spoke the word of God boldly* (Acts 4:31).

Soon after their baptism with the Spirit and their full immersion in His presence, the disciples needed to receive a refilling. The Spirit needed to come upon them again for a top-up experience.

This is the situation for all Christians. Once we receive the baptism with the Spirit, we do enter into a more empowered relationship with God, but we do not always remain on the same level of being filled with Him. At a worship service or when someone prays for us, the Holy Spirit may come in fullness and manifest His presence in an awesome way; but however great the mountain peak experience may be, we do not stay there. After every filling we need a refilling because we do not always stay on the same level of Spirit power. Our relationship with the Holy Spirit is dynamic and needs our permanent attention. God is sovereign and remains outside of our control.

The good news is that despite our constant need for top-up experiences, we can grow in the Spirit's power. On the one hand, the Bible warns us not to "grieve the Holy Spirit" (Eph. 4:30) and not to "put out the Spirit's fire" (1 Thess. 5:19); but on the other hand, the Bible encourages us to "keep in step with the Spirit" (Gal. 5:25), and the more we learn to obey this instruction, the more He can use us to achieve even greater things in Jesus' name.

Spirit power also increases in another way. When we are first baptized with the Holy Spirit, we can do whatever the Spirit prompts us to do. We may heal someone, speak a word of wisdom or prophesy, but there also seems to be another level of Spirit power where some of these spiritual manifestations become entrusted to us as spiritual gifts on a more permanent basis. The Bible keeps encouraging us to have more of the Spirit:

Now eagerly desire the greater gifts (1 Corinthians 12:31).

...eagerly desire gifts of the Spirit, especially prophecy (1 Corinthians 14:1).

...fan into flame the gift of God, which is in you through the laying on of my hands (2 Timothy 1:6).

In summary, every Christian who confesses Jesus as Lord has a measure of the Spirit's power in him, but then everyone can also experience the baptism with the Holy Spirit where there is a fuller release and infilling of the Holy Spirit in the believer. After this initial baptism with the Spirit and infilling, there needs to be refillings because the same level of the Spirit's power and manifest presence does not remain with us constantly. Furthermore, we can actually grow in the Spirit's power. Thus, we do not only receive the Holy Spirit once and then retain Him as our static possession. There is an ongoing need to be filled with the Holy Spirit and, therefore, an ongoing need to apply the spiritual principles, which will be expounded in the course of this chapter.

Repentance

We now consider the spiritual principles that make us ready to receive the Holy Spirit in the way that God has intended for us. The first and most foundational principle is the act of repentance. Before Jesus even came on the scene, another man prepared people for His coming by preaching repentance to them. John the Baptist encouraged everyone to turn away from sin and be ready for the Lord (see Mark 1:1-8). Jesus built on the work of John and further confirmed the need for repentance. There was no other way for entering into the kingdom of God; therefore, He instructed His disciples to keep preaching "repentance and forgiveness of sins...in his name to all nations" (Luke 24:47). Thus, after Jesus' ascension, the disciples clarified in their very first sermon that repentance was indeed the gateway for receiving the Holy Spirit:

*... **Repent** and be baptized, every one of you, in the name of Jesus Christ for the forgiveness of your sins. **And you will receive the gift of the Holy Spirit*** (Acts 2:38).

From the beginning, the disciples explained that, on the condition of repentance, the Holy Spirit would be given. This condition was treated as a serious matter and there was a general insistence that "without holiness no one will see the Lord" (Heb. 12:14). Throughout the Bible, the disciples kept warning people about sliding back into sin and compromise because the fullness of the Holy Spirit would not be found among unholy sin:

And do not grieve the Holy Spirit of God...Get rid of all bitterness, rage and anger, brawling and slander, along with every form of malice (Ephesians 4:30-31).

In my upbringing and my own practice as a pastor, the teaching on repentance and holiness was not a big priority. I was always quick to excuse lapses in devotion and remnants of sin because our God was loving and merciful. In my mind, He would understand and tolerate our modern church life because no one seemed to escape the consumer culture of the West.

Yet, one day I was convicted by an account in Charles Finney's autobiography. He was a skeptical lawyer who was so resistant to the Christian faith that one man said, "If you Christians can convert Finney, I will believe in religion." Thus, his conversion attracted attention and, soon after, other young men followed him and sought God in the same way as he did. For reasons of privacy, Finney had prayed for his salvation in a grove outside the village. As this became known, other young men made the same journey into the woods to pray in the privacy of a grove, and they all came back with the joy of salvation.

However, one man resisted. He reasoned that he had a home for prayer and did not need to go into the woods to make his peace with God. His story of conversion was not to be the same as others, and his pride became committed on this point. Only, God made him recognize his pride and did not relieve him of his sin. He wanted to become a Christian but could feel nothing but distress over his guilt.

The man argued with God and sought to convince God that he was not proud. At one time, he became so enraged that God did not hear his prayer that he was tempted to kill himself. The temptation was so strong that he threw away his penknife because he feared that he might use it. At another time, he returned from a meeting with more thoughts about his proud resistance to go into the woods for prayer. He again tried to prove to God that it was not pride that kept him from the grove, and he looked around for a mud puddle in which to kneel down in public. His kneeling in mud would demonstrate to God and himself that he was not proud.

This was to no avail. At long last, he gave up and went into the woods. On his return, he was shouting very loud and singing as loud as he could sing. Every few moments he would clap his hands and cry out, "I will rejoice in the God of my salvation." As soon as he had given up his point of resistance and knelt down in a grove, the Spirit of God came upon him with such power as to fill him with unspeakable joy.[2]

Reading Charles Finney's autobiography, I still remember how this testimony challenged me as a Lutheran pastor because I was certain that I would not have recognized the man's plight. My counsel to him would have been to snap out of self-condemnation and unbelief. He confessed Jesus as Lord and should now trust His mercy. Any ongoing feelings of guilt should be ignored on the basis of his sound understanding. These days, I am embarrassed about my past immaturity. A pastor must have better spiritual discernment and not assume that conversion is an automatic process that follows after saying the right words. A person's repentance is a serious matter and God insists on humble commitment before He releases the new life in the kingdom of God and the fullness of the Holy Spirit.

The Spirit Himself leads us into repentance, which then becomes a lifestyle. When Martin Luther nailed ninety-five theses for discussion to the Wittenberg church door, he not only engaged the minds of scholars but triggered the reformation of the church; his very first thesis picked up on the foundational value of repentance:

Thesis 1 (emphasis added): When our Lord and Master, Jesus Christ, said "Repent," he called for *the entire life of believers to be one of repentance.*

No individual or church will enjoy the fullness of the Holy Spirit without repentance as a commitment for life. This may sound like a serious imposition but the Holy Spirit is gentle and full of surprises. With much love, He is leading us into growing humility.

In March 2008, I sat down at my desk to write a sermon that was based on my research and notes. However, when I began writing, the sermon took on a life of its own and a completely different message was produced. I had a sense that this was God; therefore, I preached the message that confronted us Lutherans with our persistent opposition to the moves of God.

For instance, I reflected on how we had opposed the coming of Billy Graham to Australia. Church delegates from across the nation had passed the following resolution at the General Synod of 1968:

> …We cannot, however, recommend participation or cooperation of our pastors and congregations in Dr Graham's campaign. Dr Graham does not proclaim the Gospel in its truth and purity. …Participation in the preliminary prayer meetings and cooperation in the campaign can hardly avoid compromise of the truth and entanglement in unionism….

This was a mistake; even in our own ranks there are now pastors and other church members who have become Christians through the work of Billy Graham. Then I continued my sermon with our more recent opposition to the Alpha Course. In this case, we did not issue an official warning about the program, but many clergy conversations about the course were negative. We frowned at the perceived flaws of the teaching material. Even the statistics of new life and faith around the globe did not give us reason for joy.

In my preaching, further evidence of a Lutheran culture that had been opposing the moves of God was presented. We Lutherans had kept our distance to Rick Warren's 40 Days of Purpose program that swept the nation in 2004, and we also maintained a cloud of suspicion over the international Emmaus Walk, despite the joyful testimonies of Lutherans. Furthermore, we remained negative about the worship music of the Hillsong Church in Sydney even though Australian songwriters such as Darlene Zschech kept impacting the world.

With mounting evidence in my sermon, we could see that there was something in our Lutheran culture that had been resisting the moves of God. Maybe we were too proud to acknowledge anything that was not Lutheran. At the end of my sermon, I included one last piece of evidence that made the list, more or less, "by accident." I had no emotional attachment to the issue, but mentioned our Lutheran judgment of the "Toronto Blessing."

I believe that without a doubt, what God poured out on the Toronto Airport church in 1994 ranks among the most maligned movements in modern church history—and I had joined the critical voices even though I had never enquired about anything that transpired. However, in the months before I preached the sermon, I came across an audio teaching by the senior pastor of that church. This was not planned but happened as I was browsing the Internet. The teaching was good and surprised me because I had imagined this kind of pastor to be more emotional and over-the-top. Yet he was calm and solid.

This discovery challenged my prejudice, which was further eroded when I read another secondhand book and discovered it was by the same pastor. The title was *The Father's Blessing*, and I liked the book. At the very least, it proved to me that this pastor was not a "loose cannon," but a man of God. He wrote about what was happening in his church, and I learned that the experiences were not so much about the Holy Spirit but an encounter with the love of the Father.

On reflection, I recognized that I knew some of the fruit that was coming out of the Toronto Airport Church. For instance, the Alpha Course had connections to this outpouring of the Holy Spirit because a staff member had brought the "blessing" to the London church, which in time, would produce the Alpha program. Furthermore, I was familiar with American missionaries Rolland and Heidi Baker who were active in Mozambique. They had received healing and prophetic revelation in Toronto and then planted more than six thousand churches in only five years.

Without doing any more research or showing any special interest in the Toronto Blessing, I knew enough to include the phenomenon in my list of God's moves that we Lutherans kept opposing. After I finished my sermon, I invited the church members to come forward, take the microphone, and lead us in prayers of repentance. One by one, we expressed our sorrow and acknowledged our own sin and the failings of our denomination. There was no finger-pointing or superior attitude, just genuine humility.

The very next week, I went to a church conference at the Gold Coast, which was three hours away. I had no idea where we were going and who the main speaker would be. A Pentecostal friend had arranged everything, and I did not care whether the conference promised to be good or bad. I would use the time as a break and to draw near to God.

However, the worship services at the conference were blessed with an almost tangible presence of God that I had never experienced before. I received an impartation on the second night that had me lying on the carpet for the first time in my life. As I was lying on the carpet, I was further impacted by the tears I was crying. This was the first time in twenty-one years that I was shedding tears. What was happening? I had come to the conference for rest and here I was crying. The tears were also rather specific. I was grieving over our congregation and denomination and, lying on the carpet, I understood that a previous prophetic word was accurate. At a prayer meeting, one of our members had claimed that God was speaking to us the words of Revelation 3:15-20. God accused us of being lukewarm, but also promised His coming.

I was very thankful for the experience because God had touched me and spoken to me. Then I processed another piece of information. The little church that had organized the conference was in fact connected and submitted to the Toronto Airport Church. I did not even know that such a church existed in Australia but, at the conference, I began to realize that, as soon as we repented of our Lutheran judgment of the Toronto Blessing, God allowed me to step into the very stream of blessings that were flowing out of Toronto.

Before the morning service the next day, I had a "chance encounter" with the pastor who was organizing the conference. I shared with him how our Lutheran congregation repented the previous Sunday of judging the Toronto Blessing, and this week, by coming to the conference, I had already received from the outpouring that happened first at Toronto. He immediately invited me to share this testimony with the conference, and I had the chance to repent again publicly in this setting. I was not an official representative of our denomination, but I love our church and spoke as one of the pastors.

However, this was not the end of God's provisions. One month later, Pastor Peter Steicke, a Lutheran colleague and friend, was to conduct a "Father's Heart Weekend" at Living Grace. It dawned on me that this weekend was also connected to Toronto because Peter, on his return from a mission trip to Uganda, was prayed for in a church in Amsterdam, Holland. A former staff member of the Toronto Airport Church prayed for him and what Peter received was an impartation of the fatherly heart of God, which was the essence of the Toronto Blessing. As he was twice going down under the Spirit's power, he received a download of the Father's heart of love. He said that, in an instant, God impressed on him all of the Scripture passages that taught on this theme and the revelation became the seminar he would teach among us.

Thus, one Sunday we repented of opposing the moves of God and more or less "by accident" also mentioned the Toronto Blessing. Yet the Holy Spirit knew what He was doing. We needed to humble ourselves and acknowledge the truth because repentance is the gateway for receiving more from the Holy Spirit. It was not hard for us but important to Him.

Faith

The second spiritual principle, which prepares us for receiving the Spirit, is to put our faith in the promises of God. The disciples had heard Jesus promise them the baptism with the Spirit, and they believed Him. Thus, they stayed in Jerusalem until the promise had come true. We need to act with the same confidence and believe that we will also receive the Holy Spirit, according to Jesus' words.

However, this is where I encountered the greatest difficulty because I had not been adequately taught about the Holy Spirit at home or in the church. How was I to have faith in something that was unknown to me? Even the Bible asks the same question, "How can they believe in the one of whom they have not heard?" (see Rom. 10:14).

When the apostle Paul met some Christians in Ephesus, he realized that they had not yet been baptized with the Spirit. He asked them, "Did you receive the Holy Spirit when you believed?" They answered, "No, we have not even heard that there is a Holy Spirit" (Acts 19:2). They lacked faith because they had not been taught, and therefore they did not receive. This was my condition even as an ordained pastor. However, for the Christians in Ephesus, the lack of knowledge was remedied and faith implanted. The apostle Paul placed his hands on them and they received the Holy Spirit.

When we have been taught and put our faith in what we have learned, we know that God responds to us. He responds to faith. He does not demand that we advance further and earn the gift of the Spirit by our own mature efforts. The Holy Spirit is a gift and is given in response to faith. The Bible is quite clear that "without faith it is impossible to please God" (Heb. 11:6). But Jesus promised that even with "faith as small as a mustard seed…nothing will be impossible for you" (Matt. 17:20).

Faith is the key to receiving from God, but the opposite is also true. Unbelief blocks His power. For instance, in His own hometown Jesus could not do any miracles because they had no faith: "He could not do any miracles there…He was amazed at their lack of faith" (Mark 6:5-6).

For Martin Luther also, unbelief was the chief sin because it makes God out to be a liar whose promises cannot be trusted. He writes in his Large Catechism, "Where this faith is missing, there can be no proper prayer…they get nothing."[3]

It is important to God that we exercise faith and put our trust in Him. He responds when we believe that we will receive the Holy Spirit in all of His fullness. I may also add that God responds to passionate faith that engages the heart, feelings, and real desire. God is pleased by fervent faith that hungers and thirsts for Him, including the fullness of the Spirit (see also Rev. 2:4; 3:15).

As a side note, I may add that faith often involves risk, which means there is a stepping out in faith. God has a habit of revealing His will to us and then asking us to act on the revelation before any guarantee of success. For instance, He may prompt us to adopt a daring church budget before the money is in the bank. The disciples made such an experience when Jesus asked them to feed the multitudes with five loaves of bread and two fish. This was an impossible task; but as the disciples stepped out in faith and began the process of handing out the food, the loaves and fish multiplied in their hands (see Luke 9:12-17; Matt. 10:19-20).

God rewards faith. This means that sometimes we step out in faith before we have a sense of the Spirit's infilling. As soon as God speaks, we move and trust that the Spirit will be there for the given assignment.

In 2010, I was the main speaker at a church conference in Fiji, and one of my talks featured a few testimonies of God healing the blind. For the past few years, our congregation had been on the journey of believing God for more healings in our midst and there had been breakthroughs—but also disappointments. Thus, I was not exactly brimming with confidence when it came to the healing ministry. At home, I try anything because I am among the people of my own church family, but being overseas is a different matter. In Fiji, I was unknown and would be judged on the basis of only a few ministry days. It would not be a nice feeling to be exposed to another disappointment before my hosts.

However, as I entered the church to give the talk with testimonies of God healing the blind, an elderly man with dark sunglasses and a white cane was sitting in the front row of the church. I looked at him and immediately said to God, "You are setting me up. This man looks like the classical blind man. You want me to preach and then also pray for this blind man." I did not argue with God and resolved to be obedient.

After the message, I did not want to target the man directly but invited all those with eye problems to come forward for prayer. About ten people came forward but not the blind man. In fact, he removed his sunglasses and was walking to the side of the church without his cane and perfectly good eyesight. I am sure that God was enjoying this, but I only later appreciated God's sense of humor.

Since the whole congregation was watching, I did not pray long for each person. Using my thumbs, I touched the eyes of those in the healing line and then came the moment that I dreaded. I had to ask whether there was any improvement and would be embarrassed if no hands went up. However, to my surprise, about seven people raised their hands and claimed that they had received some healing. I asked the first person what had happened to him and he said that he had been blind in his left eye, but now he could see. At first, I thought that

I had misunderstood the translator because this man was quite un-emotional and any healing of blindness would surely engender greater excitement. However, the translator and the senior pastor confirmed that the claim was true. He came to the meeting with blindness in his left eye, but Jesus healed him.

I was beaming with joy, and the other testimonies were also encouraging. For instance, one woman had no longer been able to read the Bible because, in old age, her vision had become blurry and everything was out of focus. Yet, at this meeting, Jesus had healed her and she could read again. On my return to Australia, I told the testimonies in our church, and we also had one older woman who was healed of short-sightedness and gave away her glasses. Thus the healings that came out of the one worship service in Fiji were wonderful, but it took faith to pray for the healing of eyes in front of strangers. God prompted me, but then a stepping out in faith was required before the Holy Spirit would do His healing work. Faith is an important key for releasing the Spirit.

Prayer

The third spiritual principle that prepares us for receiving the Spirit is to spend time in prayer. Jesus encouraged us to persevere until the breakthrough of the Spirit's coming has happened to us:

> *…Ask and it will be given to you; seek and you will find; knock and the door will be opened to you. For everyone who asks receives; the one who seeks finds; and to the one who knocks, the door will be opened. Which of you fathers, if your son asks for a fish, will give him a snake instead? Or if he asks for an egg, will give him a scorpion? If you then, though you are evil, know how to give good gifts to your children, how much more will your Father in heaven give the Holy Spirit to those who ask him!* (Luke 11:9-13)

Sometimes there is no instant response to our prayers; but as we ask and seek and knock, we can be certain that the Holy Spirit will be given to us. In fact, everyone will receive and experience the goodness of God the Father because He is so much better than human fathers.

Jesus Himself was praying when He was being baptized with the Spirit and the same may have been true for His disciples on the day of Pentecost. As they persevered together, the Holy Spirit came upon them:

> ...*And as he was praying*, *heaven was opened and the Holy Spirit descended on him in bodily form like a dove...* (Luke 3:21-22).

> *When the day of Pentecost came,* **they were all together in one place.** *Suddenly...all of them were filled with the Holy Spirit...* (Acts 2:1-4).

Jesus' teaching on prayer is not complicated; but in my upbringing and early ministry as an ordained pastor, I had never prayed for the Holy Spirit or heard anyone else pray that the Holy Spirit may be poured out on people. However, this has changed, and I join others now in praying for the Holy Spirit. I ask Jesus, "Lord, please fill me again with the Holy Spirit."

The invitation is to pray, and we can do so with great passion that includes the discipline of fasting. Jesus assumed that, on occasion, we would fast from food and wrong priorities (see Matt. 6:16). As we allow ourselves to be stripped bare, we can test our desire and purely focus on God with passion for the Holy Spirit.

Another good discipline is to pray in unity with other Christians. Especially united prayer avails much: "Again, truly I tell you that *if two of you on earth agree about anything they ask for, it will be done for them* by my Father in heaven" (Matt. 18:19).

The Holy Spirit is attracted by Christian unity because the Holy Spirit does not just become our individual possession but is God's gift to the church as the community of Christians. The Bible identifies the entire church as the temple of the Holy Spirit and this corporate aspect of His presence continues in His purpose of seeing us serve each other with the manifestations of Himself:

> *Do you not discern and understand that you [the whole church at Corinth] are God's temple (His sanctuary), and that God's Spirit has His permanent dwelling in you [to be at home in you,*

collectively as a church and also individually]? (1 Corinthians 3:16 Amplified Bible)

Now to each one the manifestation of the Spirit is given for the common good (1 Corinthians 12:7).

United prayer avails much because the Holy Spirit wants to take residence not only in individuals but in the community of Christians for mutual service and united mission. When we pray together, the Spirit will come.

Impartation

The fourth principle for receiving the Holy Spirit has to do with impartation. Apparently the Holy Spirit can be passed on from one person to another, usually through the laying on of hands. The first immersion in the Spirit may happen in this way, but there is also the ongoing practice of imparting spiritual gifts through the laying on of hands:

Then Peter and John placed their hands on them, and they re-ceived the Holy Spirit...the Spirit was given at the laying on of the apostles' hands... (Acts 8:17-18; see also Acts 19:6).

I long to see you so that I may impart to you some spiritual gift... (Romans 1:11; see also 2 Timothy 1:6).

It is a great privilege that we can serve each other with the Holy Spirit. As we cooperate with Him and in obedience place our hands on others, He comes upon people and releases His gifts.

However, in the past, I objected to this idea because I did not want to be dependent on anyone else. Why would I need to seek out special people and receive from them what God had granted to them? I did not want to jump on the bandwagon of someone else's anointing. Yet God dealt with my pride, and now I try to be the first in line for impartation.

Over the years, God has arranged numerous people to pray for me with the laying on of hands. However, the person I valued most for impartation was the American missionary Heidi Baker. I had been watching and listening to her preaching on the Internet. For more than a year, I was receiving through her as I immersed myself in one conference recording after another. There were lessons on healings and miracles; but most of all, I wanted to fall in love with God like she had fallen in love with Him. She was preaching from a place that I did not know. There were many rich hours of touching something new in God through her sermons before the computer screen.

Then I found out that Heidi and her husband would be coming to the Gold Coast in 2010. I was the first to register and was quite anxious that my wife and oldest daughter would also get tickets. My family and congregation knew how excited I was, and they began teasing me. My daughters suggested that I should write a fan letter. Yet, I did not care. My interest was not so much in the teaching content of the conference, because I had already heard and read so much. What I wanted more than anything was that Heidi Baker would pray for me. I desired an impartation and, for this purpose, I fasted two days before the conference.

The first session was on a Wednesday night, but the announcement came that Heidi Baker would not speak before Friday night. Two more days of waiting were difficult. On Friday afternoon, we had to pick up our oldest daughter Dominique from a bus station at 5:30 PM. From there it would be a half an hour drive to the conference center where the session was scheduled to begin at 7 PM. This would be Heidi's first segment. However, as we were waiting for her, Dominique rang us to say that her bus had a flat tyre and that she would be one and a half hours late. This meant that her arrival time would be 7 PM—the time of Heidi Baker's first session.

I was beginning to stress and my wife struggled to calm my nerves. Dominique arrived at 7, and without even saying hello, I made her run to the car, suppressed any small talk, and made sure that we did not get lost on the way to the center. At the entrance of the center, a friend from our church was waiting. I had no time for any greeting, so he and others quickly ushered me to a good seat. They were still playing songs, and Heidi was worshiping about two meters away.

After she finished preaching, it was time for pastors to receive prayer. Other groups had already been called up and occupied a fair measure of the extensive stage area, but there was still space in front of Heidi. I was quick and bold and managed to be the first pastor kneeling right in front of her. However, she invited those under the age of twenty-five to pray for the pastors and proceeded to pray for the pastor next to me.

A young woman prayed for me. She had a prophetic word for me and encouraged me to speak out what was weighing me down because this would bring me relief; but her prophetic word seemed to miss the mark. Usually I am patient with those who are trying out spiritual gifts, but with Heidi being so close, I was not in the frame of mind to be patient. Yet the young woman persisted with her discernment and the whole experience began to irritate me.

Behind me, a young man began praying for me and he kept pushing into my back. Other pastors to my left were overcome with energetic laughter, which made them roll around and hold their bellies. They kept bumping into me with their full body weight. I looked at them and thought that this was not what I wanted. Heidi is carrying a deposit of the Spirit for nations. Why then would anyone be satisfied with a "tickle anointing"?

I am not usually feeling this kind of irritation, but the young woman in front of me kept talking about my "burden." The young man behind me kept pushing into my back, and the pastors to my left kept bumping into me. This was not going well, and I realized that Heidi was moving in another direction. There were more pastors behind us, and I saw no longer any reason to occupy my place on the stage. I got up and walked away. I was fighting disappointment. God had obviously not wanted Heidi Baker to pray for me. I reminded myself that God was always good and processed the experience. At least, I would not have to blame myself for a lack of boldness and initiative. I had done everything humanly possible, but it was not meant to be.

When I arrived at the side of the stage, I caught up with our evangelist, David Challenor, and shared only briefly my disappointment. He asked me whether I had prayed about this and I assured him that I had.

The next thing I remember is seeing Heidi walking across the stage toward me. David had gone to find her and asked her to pray for his pastor. Heidi had agreed and proceeded to follow David across the entire length of the stage that was cramped with people wanting ministry from her.

I could not believe what was happening and in a few words explained to Heidi Baker that I was a Lutheran pastor and shared some of my journey that was impacted by her preaching. She hugged me and gave me her full, loving attention. She asked for my wife, Tatjana, and I waved to her so that she and my daughter could join us on the stage. Heidi hugged them also, and then we were kneeling opposite each other.

Heidi prayed and prophesied for about fifteen minutes, being oblivious to everyone else. She prayed intensely about ministering into the Lutheran family. After a while, the Holy Spirit moved on me, and I began sobbing with my body shaking.

Heidi's prayer was picking up on my persistent passion for the Lutheran church tribe. Even though I am keen and free to minister in any setting, my heart has a soft spot for the millions of Lutherans who do not yet know that there is more in God. Heidi kept praying about bringing "fresh bread" and "fresh wine" to the Lutherans and she communicated to us a prophetic vision. There would be a harvest.

After the prayer, Heidi gave Dominique a long hug and kissed her on the forehead. Dominique told her, "Dad is so excited to meet you." Heidi answered, "And I am so excited meeting him."

During the whole ministry time, all the attending members of Living Grace had gathered around us and were also laying hands on us while Heidi was praying. However, when Heidi had finished, she asked us to pray for her. Heidi was not at all in a rush. Finally, her personal assistant came and reminded her that she needed to go.

The whole experience was "miraculous" in the sense that it was so much more than I had hoped for. When I had done everything that was in my power and failed, God began to move in His power. I had desired impartation; then received more than anyone else at the conference. Tatjana was healed from a wounded heart in the prayer time with Heidi. The years of ministry had been hard and she had been paying a price; but after prayer, she was a new woman and everyone noticed.

The encouragement is to receive the Holy Spirit through the prayer of others and the laying on of hands. We can serve each other in the community of the church that is the temple of the Spirit.

Waiting

The fifth spiritual principle, which prepares us for receiving the Spirit, is the simple instruction to wait. Jesus told His first disciples to stay in the city of Jerusalem until the Holy Spirit was poured out on them (see Luke 24:49; Acts 1:4-5). There was a delay, and after a number of days the waiting disciples received the promised Holy Spirit. Soon after the first outpouring of the Spirit, another delay confronted the new converts in Samaria. It was only after Peter and John came from Jerusalem and prayed for them that they were being baptized with the Spirit. Sometimes, for whatever reason, there is a waiting period before the Holy Spirit comes.

One of our church members kept coming to one Holy Spirit seminar after another for two years and could not get a breakthrough. She did receive the gift of tongues at the very first seminar, but simply could not sense God's love for her. She became depressed; but two years later, she felt immersed in God's love for the first time and said, "It is like going from black-and-white photography to color." Why was there a time delay in being satisfied in the Spirit? In her case, I believe that she was being baptized with the Spirit early on; therefore, I assured her that she could simply accept the gift by faith. Her experience was not dependent on emotions. In my estimate, she had a more general problem in relating to anyone with trust and openness. There was an inner wound that made it hard for her to be vulnerable—even with God. This affected her emotional freedom and did not allow her to sense the love of God.

In my understanding, this case points to possible time delays in enjoying the fullness of the Spirit because of personal issues. This one church member had inner wounds that needed healing. Also, there was one Sunday when a demon manifested in her and was expelled. Other people may not struggle with inner wounds but nurse hidden sins, which also quench the Spirit's operation in them. Yet to make this quite clear, the first disciples in Jerusalem and Samaria suffered more fundamental time delays, which had nothing to do with them. They were simply to wait for the Spirit and the first immersion in the Spirit because God had ordained the waiting period.

Likewise, a pastor became convinced that he needed to be baptized with the Spirit and he committed himself to seek the experience. There was much prayer, Bible study, and reading books but no breakthrough. Two years later, a "chance" meeting with a missionary and a short prayer made him burst forth with spontaneous praise. There was a feeling as if waves of electricity passed through his body and the sensation of being overwhelmed by God's love. In his case, nothing had been lacking in him; God had determined to let him wait for the Spirit.[4]

However, why would God let anyone wait for the Spirit? Why would some be baptized with the Spirit when they do not even want the experience while others are seeking desperately but go home unfulfilled? Some suggest that the waiting period is good for character formation and is also dealing with human pride. As we exercise desperate faith, our desire and devotion are tested and we are humbled by our complete lack of control. We learn to trust God and not turn against him with an offended heart.

Furthermore, Jesus Himself taught His disciples before the baptism with the Holy Spirit. When the Holy Spirit comes, He can be a big distraction to any clear thinking. There may be signs and wonders, healings, and overwhelming joy. This can mess with anyone's head. Thus, the time of waiting can be a good preparation time of getting insights into the Word of God and building solid foundations for dealing with the Spirit's power when it comes.

While we wait, it is of the utmost importance that we watch our attitude. There is no reason to become despondent or doubt the gift-character of the Spirit. We are not to run ourselves down as the most undeserving Christians who are simply not worthy enough to receive the baptism with the Spirit. No one can earn the Spirit or demand the Spirit as reward for personal righteousness because no one ever measures up to God's perfect standard of holiness. It is on account of God's goodness that we receive the fullness of the Spirit and, according to His promise, everyone will receive.

There is one practical encouragement flowing out of this. We keep praying about the Spirit and we keep receiving prayer for the infilling of the Spirit. We never give up responding to opportunities for prayer. The promised breakthrough will come in time.

Two Closing Remarks

How do people know that they have received the infilling or refilling of the Holy Spirit? This is easy to answer—when they begin to speak in tongues, prophesy, feel incredible joy and love, tingle all over the body and experience other physical manifestations. However, not everyone is impacted in their emotions and body. One pastor's wife, who had an amazing healing gift, never felt anything when she prayed for healing. She simply exercised faith and prayed in obedience. However, the outcome was undeniable. The sick were recovering.

In your own life, you may want to check whether the Holy Spirit has produced any fruit such as love, joy, patience, peace, kindness, goodness, faithfulness, gentleness, and self-control (see Gal. 5:22-23). This kind of fruit does not always come with ecstatic outbursts but may come with more steady emotions of love, joy, and peace. Furthermore, you may want to check whether you can sense the Holy Spirit communicating with you because "those who are led by the Spirit of God are the children of God" (Rom. 8:14) and "the Spirit himself testifies with our spirit that we are God's children" (Rom. 8:16). If you cannot discern much fruit and are not sure about the Spirit leading you, then it could be that you can expect a greater infilling of the Spirit. Maybe it will be your first time.

There is another question. Could it be that in some cases the baptism with the Spirit is not just one big decisive event but happens more gradually over time? Most people in our church can pinpoint the time and date of their Spirit baptism, but this is not the case with me. In my life, there was an extended season of renewal and the Spirit filling me. As far as I know, His fullness was not poured out in one breakthrough event. This is also the experience of children who grow up as Christians. Many of them seem to grow in the fullness of the Spirit as they grow in maturity.

Jesus' wonderful promise is that everyone who is asking the Father will receive the Spirit. In this chapter, were listed five spiritual principles that make us ready to receive the Holy Spirit in the way that God has intended for us. These five keys to the baptism with the Spirit have to do with 1) repentance, 2) faith, 3) prayer, 4) impartation, and 5) waiting.

ENDNOTES

1. See also John 20:21-23.

2. Garth M. Rosell and Richard A.G. Dupuis, eds., *Charles Finney: Original Memoirs of Charles G. Finney* (Grand Rapids, MI: Zondervan, 1989), 25-27.

3. Friedemann Hebart, *Martin Luther: Luther's Large Catechism, Anniversary Translation and Introductory Essay* (Adelaide, Australia: Lutheran Publishing House, 1983), 162.

4. Charles Ringma, "The Disquieting Presence of the Spirit," *Church on Fire*, Geoff Waugh, ed. (Melbourne, Australia: JBCE, 1991), 41-42.

Chapter 4

Will You Still Serve Him?

THE HOLY SPIRIT AND SUFFERING

Jesus was a person "full of the Holy Spirit" (Luke 4:1), and He told everyone, "The Spirit of the Lord is on me" (Luke 4:18). Peter, one of the disciples who witnessed most of His work, later said about Jesus:

> *You know what has happened throughout the province of Judea, beginning in Galilee after the baptism that John preached—* ***how God anointed Jesus of Nazareth with the Holy Spirit and*** ***power,*** *and how he went around doing good and healing all who were under the power of the devil, because God was with him* (Acts 10:37-38).

There was absolutely nothing wrong with Jesus. On the contrary, He demonstrated what it meant to be anointed with the Spirit and power. He showcased how to be full of the Spirit and do great things.

Only one key detail of His life did not seem to fit the picture— He suffered and died. How was this possible? In the presence of so much Spirit power, how can there be weakness, broken bones, tears and blood, rejection and ridicule, even torture and death? It was bad enough that Jesus was a poor peasant from the country who failed to be recognized by the governing elite. However, His violent execution on a cross proved to be too much for His disciples. They could not cope. How can a man, full of the Spirit, be such an apparent failure?

When Jesus rose from the dead, He faced this question and took great pains to explain that even the Christ, who was anointed with the Spirit, had to suffer and die. He had reasoned with His disciples previously; therefore somewhat exasperated, He charged His disciples with impatient words:

> *How foolish you are, and how slow to believe all that the prophets have spoken!* **Did not the Messiah have to suffer these things and then enter his glory?** (Luke 24:25-26)

Why did Jesus have to suffer? Was it really necessary? Chances are that Christians in general are slow to believe that there is indeed a connection between Spirit power on the one hand and suffering and death on the other. Yet, it was Jesus' very own pain and death that made Him worthy to receive even more power than before:

> *...***You are worthy** *to take the scroll and to open its seals,* **because you were slain,** *and with your blood you purchased for God persons from every tribe and language and people and nation* (Revelation 5:9).

The Power Problem

Before we come back to Jesus' own experiences, we will tackle the connection between Spirit power and suffering from another angle. Apostle Paul wrote to one of his congregations that they were full of the Spirit and in full possession of all Spirit power. He assured them with these words, "you do not lack any spiritual gift" (1 Cor. 1:7). Yet, almost in the same breath, Paul confronted them with severe shortcomings in their Christian life:

> *...***I could not address you as people who live by the Spirit** *but as people who are still worldly—mere infants in Christ. ...For since there is jealousy and quarrelling among you, are you not worldly?...* (1 Corinthians 3:1-3).

In addition to jealousy and quarrelling, Paul identified additional blemishes in their conduct and chided them about moral failures that were not compatible with the *Holy* Spirit. The Corinthians had to own up to church divisions, incest, mixing with sexually impure Christians, lawsuits within the church, corrupt communion practices, disregard for the poor, denial of the resurrection, pride and boasting (see 1 Cor. 3:1-9; 5:1-11; 6:1-8; 11:1-24; 15:12-19).

It is fascinating that, despite this long list of shameful behavior, Paul still maintained that these Christians were not lacking any spiritual gifts. According to him, in this church all of the spiritual gifts remained in operation with the questionable outcome that, in the midst of sin, there was the spectacle of supernatural wisdom, faith, healings, miracles, prophecy, distinguishing between spirits, and speaking in tongues. This must have been confusing for many Christians. How can the Spirit flourish in these sinful conditions? Is this not bringing spiritual gifts into disrepute? Paul was well aware of this problem; therefore, he pleaded with the Corinthians always to combine spiritual gifts with love:

> *If I speak in the tongues of men or of angels, but do not have love, I am only a resounding gong or a clanging cymbal. If I have the gift of prophecy and can fathom all mysteries and all knowledge, and if I have a faith that can move mountains, but do not have love, I am nothing. If I give all I possess to the poor and give over my body to hardship that I may boast, but do not have love, I gain nothing* (1 Corinthians 13:1-3).

This seems to have been the problem. The Corinthians may have spoken in the tongues of angels and fathomed mysteries and knowledge through the gift of prophecy. They may have accomplished other great feats in the power of the Spirit, but without love, this was not attractive to anyone. What is more, the exercise of all spiritual gifts without love gained them nothing, and they remained nothing in God's eyes.

Apostle Paul offered them correction. Power without love is not an option. It is selfish and proud. God always meant for His power to be in the service of love, and this is what He demonstrated in Jesus who came to seek and save the lost. Yet for us the problem remains. Modern Christians often resemble the Corinthians at their worst because power corrupts easily and much is given even to brand-new Christians. Since the baptism with the Spirit is not tied to maturity, any recent convert may be immersed in the power of the Spirit and then prophesy or do other mighty works in God's name (see Acts 19:6). How will this power not corrupt the brand-new believer? This is the problem.

The Wounding from the Beginning

Frequently God meets the problem of too much power with a dose of suffering, which is building character, and this marks the Christian life from the beginning. Whenever a person comes to faith and experiences the power of salvation, there is also suffering. When the apostle Peter preached his first sermon after Jesus had ascended to heaven, he had a confronting message:

> *Fellow Israelites, listen to this: Jesus of Nazareth was a man accredited by God to you by miracles, wonders and signs, which God did among you through him, as you yourselves know. This man was handed over to you by God's deliberate plan and foreknowledge; and you, with the help of wicked men, put him to death by nailing him to the cross. But God raised him from the dead, freeing him from the agony of death, because it was impossible for death to keep its hold on him. …be assured of this: God has made this Jesus, whom you crucified, both Lord and Messiah* (Acts 2:22-36).

This message was putting pressure on the congregation. The charge was that the people were guilty of innocent blood and had rebelled against God. They had crucified Jesus even though they had witnessed how He had been endorsed by God through miracles, wonders and signs. Now, as proclaimed by the Spirit-filled disciples, God had raised Jesus from the dead and made Him their Lord and Messiah. They would have to reconsider their deeds. Would they now accept the One they had murdered on a cross?

This was not an easy-going sermon, but the crowd came under conviction. They began to feel badly about the past and their crime. The truth began to hurt them; and according to the Bible, "they were cut to the heart" (Acts 2:37).

This experience of being "cut to the heart" was not enjoyable. It was the kind of suffering that awaits every new believer at the time of conversion. There is the pain of having one's eyes opened and seeing the truth that comes with weeping over sin. There is the pain of realizing that our human achievements count for nothing before God—and we all depend absolutely on the blood of Jesus for forgiveness. This humbles us and renders us helpless. At our conversion, our pride is cut down and we are hurting in the act of repentance; but this achieves for us the power of salvation and eternal rejoicing.

John Bunyan, pastor and author, made this point strongly in one of his books, "Conversion is not the smooth, easy-going process some men seem to think…It is wounding work, of course, this breaking of the hearts, but without wounding there is no saving…."[1]

Thus, right at the beginning of our Christian faith, God saw fit to temper the power of salvation with suffering. This means that, from the start, we find the dynamic whereby God employs suffering to humble us before releasing His power.

Suffering Progress

Apostle Paul experienced in his own life the correlation between great power and intense suffering, and he explained the connection:

> *To keep me from becoming conceited because of these surpassingly great revelations, there was given me a thorn in my flesh, a messenger of Satan, to torment me. Three times I pleaded with the Lord to take it away from me. But he said to me, "My grace is sufficient for you, for my power is made perfect in weakness." Therefore I will boast all the more gladly about my weaknesses, so that Christ's power may rest on me. That is why, for Christ's sake, I delight in weaknesses, in insults, in hardships, in persecutions, in difficulties. For when I am weak, then I am strong* (2 Corinthians 12:7-10 NIV 1984).

As he understood the circumstances, the apostle Paul was to endure his "thorn in the flesh" because it kept him "from becoming conceited." Since God had given him "surpassingly great revelations," Paul needed the pain of many weaknesses to keep him safe from pride. At first he prayed about healing and the removal of the thorn; but in the end, he humbled himself and accepted any kind of suffering for the greater release of God's power in his life.

Paul could make sense of his suffering, and the discomfort may not have lasted for long. It is conceivable that, in time, God removed the thorn in Paul's flesh because this kind of suffering was no longer needed to keep him humble. This is what many Christians have experienced.

In the Bible, there is also David, the shepherd boy, who was the youngest son of an insignificant family and clan. One day the prophet Samuel paid a visit to David's house and surprised everyone by anointing him to be king. From the day of his anointing, "the Spirit of the Lord came powerfully upon David" (1 Sam. 16:13). He was eventually promoted to live at the royal court where he served King Saul as an armor-bearer and musician. When he defeated the giant Goliath, he became a national hero and married the king's daughter who loved him. What is more, the king's son became his closest friend and supported him. Everything was going fine. His whole life seemed to consist of one fantastic dream-run where the presence of the Spirit made everything possible. David seemed unstoppable. He was positioned to ascend the throne.

Only God had other ideas. The dream-run would be cut short and kingship would elude him for many years. David had to run for his life because the king, his father-in-law, became jealous of his growing fame and divine favor. Living in caves and desolate places, he was separated from his wife and then learned that the king, her father, had given her into marriage again to another man. This was not right and not fair. David was innocent.

At one time, David was so desperate that he sought refuge in the very hometown of Goliath, the giant whom he had killed in battle. There, he was forced to feign insanity with spit dribbling down his beard. The years on the run were hard (see 1 Sam. 21:10-13).

At another time, he returned to his place of refuge, only to find every home burned and destroyed. Then he discovered that the enemy raiders had also stolen his two wives and the families of his men. The circumstances could not get any worse and the suffering continued.

However, this furnace of testing trials served a purpose and formed David's character for kingship. Instead of turning against God and giving in to bitterness, he drew closer to God and learned ongoing encouragement in worship and praise. He was getting ready to lead a nation through adversity (see 1 Sam. 30:4-6).

The years of hardship made David draw closer to God. He did not grow bitter; and remarkably, he also retained a soft heart toward the king, his father-in-law, who was the agent of all injustice and persecution.

David was getting ready to reign with a pure heart. Twice David seemed to have the good fortune of having the king at his mercy, but twice David refrained from killing him. He accepted that it was God who was demoting and promoting leaders (see 1 Sam. 26:9-11).

David passed the tests of leadership. He would not take matters into his own hands; he would remain obedient to God in all circumstances. In the end, David mourned, wept, and fasted when Saul did not survive a battle against the Philistines. He mourned his persecutor, and thus confirmed that he was a man after God's own heart (see 1 Sam. 13:14). Kingship would be his. The fiery trials would have an end, and the anointing on him would manifest in his reign with authority.

Thus the life of David again illustrates the connection between Spirit power and suffering. God employs suffering to prepare His people and build up their character so they can wield great power without giving in to corruption and selfish pride.

At one time, God led an entire nation through this experience. He humbled and tested His people in the wilderness for forty years so they would learn to depend on God for everything and not forget Him later among the riches of the Promised Land. God used hunger and deprivations to build the character of a nation so His people would have the discipline of enjoying a greater release of His mercy and power without becoming corrupted:

> *Be careful to follow every command I am giving you today, so that you may live and increase and may enter and possess the land the Lord promised on oath to your ancestors. **Remember how the Lord your God led you all the way in the wilderness these forty years, to humble and test you in order to know what was in your heart, whether or not you would keep his commands. He humbled you, causing you to hunger and then feeding you with manna, which neither you nor your ancestors had known, to teach you that man does not live on bread alone but on every word that comes from the mouth of the Lord. Your clothes did not wear out and your feet did not swell during these forty years. Know then in your heart that as a man disciplines his son, so the Lord your God disciplines you.***

Observe the commands of the Lord your God, walking in obedience to him and revering him. For the Lord your God is bringing you into a good land—a land with brooks, streams, and deep springs gushing out into the valleys and hills; a land with wheat and barley, vines and fig trees, pomegranates, olive oil and honey; a land where bread will not be scarce and you will lack nothing; a land where the rocks are iron and you can dig copper out of the hills. When you have eaten and are satisfied, praise the Lord your God for the good land he has given you. Be careful that you do not forget the Lord your God...

He led you through the vast and dreadful wilderness, that thirsty and waterless land, with its venomous snakes and scorpions. He brought you water out of hard rock. He gave you manna to eat in the wilderness, something your ancestors had never known, to humble and test you so that in the end it might go well with you. *You may say to yourself, "My power and the strength of my hands have produced this wealth for me." But remember the Lord your God, for it is he who gives you the ability to produce wealth, and so confirms his covenant, which he swore to your ancestors...* (Deuteronomy 8:1-20).

God is still working on individuals and communities in the same way. He employs times in the wilderness and suffering to get us ready for a greater release of His power and favor. For instance, John Bunyan wrote the book *The Pilgrim's Progress* (1678), which has been translated into more than two hundred languages and is probably, next to the Bible, the most popular book ever published. Yet this success came with a price tag. The book was written in prison where over twelve years John Bunyan learned absolute surrender to God. In his autobiography, he explained how he survived. He quoted Second Corinthians 1:9, "Indeed, we felt we had received the sentence of death. But this happened that we might not rely on ourselves but on God, who raises the dead."

Then he wrote:

By this scripture I was made to see that if ever I would suffer rightly, I must first pass a sentence of death upon everything that can be properly called a thing of this life, even to reckon myself, my wife, my children, my health, my enjoyment, and all, as dead to me, and myself as dead to them. The second was, to live upon God that is invisible, as Paul said in another place; the way not to faint, is to "look not at the things which are seen, but at the things which are not seen; for the things which are seen are temporal, but the things which are not seen are eternal."[2] (See Second Corinthians 4:18.)

We can all agree that the Bible teaches us not to rely on ourselves but on God. Yet in prison, John Bunyan learned the radical nature of this proposition and passed "a sentence of death upon everything that can be properly called a thing of this life." He reckoned himself, his wife, his children, his health, his enjoyment, and all, as dead to him—and himself as dead to them. In this way, he shared the experience of Second Corinthians 1:9 and also matched the more radical words of the apostle Paul who wrote in Galatians 6:14, "May I never boast except in the cross of our Lord Jesus Christ, through which the world has been crucified to me, and I to the world."

John Bunyan came to value Jesus to the exclusion of everything else. He passed a sentence of death upon the world and considered himself as dead to everything that can be properly called a thing of this life. Thus, he survived his suffering by living for Jesus alone. However, as he passed a sentence of death upon everything that he loved, God passed a sentence of life on his pen and book. Out of the discipline in prison came the power of a best-selling book.

God may not always discipline people in the same way, but He does use suffering to break down human pride so that His greater power can operate unhindered in humble servants. In my own life, I did not expect suffering in the ministry. I was young and strong-willed. In my opinion, there would always be a way forward. Full of energy, I believed in what I was doing and was not shy in confronting opposition. I even seemed to be thriving on conflict. The mind worked better under pressure, and I had disciplined my emotions. Yet in the end, there was more conflict than ever anticipated, and it persisted for many years. As I was getting older, I discovered that I was not invincible, and I was grieving over the waste of strained relationships. In addition, the workload took its own toll because new initiatives take extra energy.

However, God allowed the pressure cooker of church tensions and busy church life to weaken me and soften me. I learned to forgive, and I learned to depend on God. Then, in my case, God seemed to take extra care in making sure that any breakthroughs would also come in a weakened state.

When the first young woman gave her heart to God, I was the one praying with her, but it was after a long day of ministry, and I was absolutely exhausted. The young woman struggled for a while to find the right words with God. Therefore, I encouraged her to come to God on another day because I felt that I could not last much longer. However, she did not want to leave and found the joy of salvation a few minutes later. This should have also been a fantastic experience for me as a pastor, but I could not savor the moment. I felt sick.

In the same way, when the first three people were falling to the floor under the power of the Spirit and the first deliverance from a demon happened, I was too exhausted to have any joyful emotion over anything. I remember thinking at one time, *God, when do You actually allow me to enjoy the ministry?* My wife, who was on her own journey, kept saying, "God will give you the desire of your heart, when you no longer want it." Thus, in our lives also, God was making sure that we, like John Bunyan, would "pass a sentence of death on everything that can be properly called a thing of this life" before He would empower us.

Then we came into a season where both us were not able to sleep properly for two years. In our desperation, we even spent some nights in separate bedrooms so that our combined tossing and turning would not make the situation worse for the other. Yet, we could not find rest, which for me meant that I was burning out. We inquired whether it was a spiritual attack, and some of our prayer people thought that it might be.

As such, in the crucial year of 2008, which marked the end of our transition into the things of the Spirit, I was in a weakened state. At the very time that God was asking the congregation whether He was allowed to come in, I was struggling to hold my concentration at meetings. In the end, I was not able to control anything and had to let God take charge; and by His grace, He preserved the church and me. More than that, He released us and provided for us.

Furthermore, a few months into the following year, without changing diet or anything else, both my wife and I were sleeping again. Our strength was coming back, and we have never again experienced this type of sleeplessness. It seems that God wanted us weak in 2008 so that He could do whatever He wanted in His power—not ours.

The principle holds true. God often uses suffering to break down our own power so that we would rely on His. He is committed to building up our character so that we have a foundation of humility before the release of His power, which so easily corrupts our worship of God.

Lessons from Jesus

When He was about thirty years old (see Luke 3:23), Jesus was being baptized with the Spirit; and He immediately experienced the three main benefits of 1) assurance, 2) victory over sin, and 3) power for mission work. From Jesus' own experience, we will learn how these three main benefits are connected with each other and facilitate the progression from suffering to power.

1. Jesus was being assured of His identity when the voice of God spoke to Him:

    *...And as he was praying, heaven was opened and the Holy Spirit descended on him in bodily form like a dove. And a voice came from heaven: "**You are my Son, whom I love; with you I am well pleased**" (Luke 3:21-22).*

2. After the voice of God spoke to Him, Jesus returned from His baptism to battle satan for forty days and remain victorious:

    *Jesus, **full of the Holy Spirit**, left the Jordan and was led by the Spirit into the wilderness, **where for forty days he was tempted by the devil**... (Luke 4:1-2).*

3. Following His victory over satan, Jesus declared that the Holy Spirit had come upon Him for power in mission work:

    *Jesus returned to Galilee in the power of the Spirit...and on the Sabbath day he went into the synagogue...and the scroll of the prophet Isaiah was handed to him. Unrolling it, he found the place where it is written: "**The Spirit of the Lord is on me, because he has anointed me to proclaim good news to the poor. He*** *has sent me to proclaim freedom for the prisoners and recovery of sight for the blind, to set the oppressed free, to proclaim the year of the Lord's favor."…He began by saying to them, "Today this scripture is fulfilled in your hearing"* (Luke 4:14-21).

Jesus received all of the three main benefits of the Spirit baptism; and according to the biblical record, the assurance of His sonship came first because He needed the assurance of His identity before He could prevail for forty days in the intense battle with satan. As He was being baptized with the Spirit, Jesus heard more clearly than ever before that He was the beloved Son of His Father in heaven, and God told Him that He was pleased with Him. With this kind of assurance, Jesus was fortified against satan who would precisely attack His identity as God's Son.

Again and again, satan would tempt Jesus with the suggestion that He needed to prove His identity. Why would the Son of God have to suffer hunger and deprivation in the wilderness? Satan reasoned with Jesus that if He was the Son of God, then He should do something that was measuring up to His status. He should secure bread for His hunger and then also power and fame.

The devil would not cease attacking Jesus over His identity. He tested Jesus with the same suggestion over forty days:

The devil said to him, "If you are the Son of God, tell this stone to become bread" (Luke 4:3).

The devil led him to Jerusalem and had him stand on the highest point of the temple. "If you are the Son of God," he said, "throw yourself down from here" (Luke 4:9).

If Jesus had not received assurances of His sonship in His Spirit baptism, He would not have had the strength to withstand satan's attacks. However, because He was "full of the Spirit," He would not doubt the Father's love. He had no need to seek validation and self-worth elsewhere.

For Jesus, the battle with satan was intense and painful; but as He was being baptized with the Spirit, He prevailed—and the kind of character was formed in Him that could now handle the Spirit's power for mission. Jesus had entered the time of temptation "full of the Holy Spirit" (Luke 4:1), but returned from the battle experience "in the power of the Spirit" (Luke 4:14). Thus, like so many Christians after Him, Jesus had learned the discipline of remaining obedient to God even in times of deprivation. He had passed the test and would not use the glory of Spirit power for His own self.

The lesson for us is to recognize again the suffering that prepares for power, and we may also take note of how important the gift of assurance was for Jesus. If He needed to be baptized with the Spirit for a deeper confidence in His sonship, then every Christian must experience the same for the testing and power that are going to come.

I close this chapter with another Bible passage that connects Jesus' own suffering with His power. We learn from Him and accept the same discipline:

> *During the days of Jesus' life on earth, he offered up prayers and petitions with fervent cries and tears to the one who could save him from death, and he was heard because of his reverent submission. **Son though he was, he learned obedience from what he suffered and, once made perfect, he became the source of eternal salvation** for all who obey him and was designated by God to be high priest in the order of Melchizedek* (Hebrews 5:7-10).

ENDNOTES

1. John Bunyan, *The Excellency of a Broken Heart,* quoted in John Piper's *Tested by Fire* (Leicester, England: Inter-Varsity Press, 2001), 65.

2. John Bunyan, *Grace Abounding to the Chief of Sinners* (Hertfordshire, England: Evangelical Press 1978), 122.

Chapter 5

The Foolishness Continues

THE MANIFESTATIONS OF THE HOLY SPIRIT

Would God ever do anything that would offend us? Would God ever upset good Christians on purpose? This has not been my expectation; therefore, as a pastor I have always tried to portray God as nice and gentle because people want to be coaxed into a relationship with Him. God is supposed to attract us with sensitive love. Yet, there is another side of Him. By design and on purpose God plans to offend and scandalize us.

The problem most church people have is that we do not always recognize God's troubling intentions because we have become used to some of His offensiveness and then do not expect any further outrage. From the comfort of today's vantage point, we look at the provocative nature of the Christian message and declare ourselves to be unaffected. With academic interest, we marvel at how other people in the Bible have always taken offense at Jesus.

People questioned His place of origin and asked, "Nazareth! Can anything good come from there?" (John 1:46). They scorned His sharing meals with suspect people and said, "Here is a glutton and drunkard, a friend of tax collectors and sinners" (Luke 7:34). They objected to His power over sickness and demons and made this claim, "It is only by Beelzebul, the prince of demons, that this fellow drives out demons" (Matt. 12:24). People objected to His preaching, and even Jesus' own disciples struggled so that He was compelled to ask them, "Does this offend you?" (John 6:61).

Much about Jesus seemed offensive. He was a wining and dining healer and preacher from Nazareth who managed to upset people all of His life and then made His own death the worst offense. Instead of reigning in glory, He claimed to be a crucified Savior, and His followers continued with the same message. They preached that power flowed from the tool of torture that was the cross of His death. This was hardly acceptable to anyone, but Jesus' followers stood their ground. The apostle Paul wrote in the Bible:

> *For the message of the cross is foolishness to those who are perishing…God was pleased through the foolishness of what was preached to save those who believe. Jews demand signs and Greeks look for wisdom, but we preach Christ crucified: a stumbling block to Jews and foolishness to Gentiles…***For the foolishness of God is wiser than human wisdom**, *and the weakness of God is stronger than human strength* (1 Corinthians 1:18-25).

In the time of the early church, people kept stumbling over the apparent foolishness of the cross, but our problem today is that we have accommodated ourselves to the message and are no longer offended by anything that Jesus has done. Today, we love the underdog who took on the religious establishment, and His cross has now become golden around our necks and on church walls. We have become used to Jesus; and with some pride, look back over centuries of church history. Yet, God does not give up so quickly in offending us; therefore, He also keeps employing more current means for disconcerting good Christians. For instance, the Bible reflects His ongoing tendency to work through people whom others judge objectionable:

> *…Not many of you were wise by human standards; not many were influential; not many were of noble birth.* **But God chose the foolish things** *of the world to shame the wise; God chose the weak things of the world to shame the strong. God chose the lowly things of this world and the despised things—and the things that are not—to nullify the things that are, so that no one may boast before him* (1 Corinthians 1:26-29).

Thus, even in our most recent history, some of the best and most effective preachers did not seem to have the right pedigree. A case in point is Charles Spurgeon who was called the "prince of preachers" but never attended any Bible college. Through different means, first Jesus and then His followers have caused other people to take offense—this was God's intention because He "chose the foolish things of the world to shame the wise." His aim was "to nullify the things that are," and His aim has not changed. God is still in the business of shaming the wise and strong. Therefore, we better be prepared. Both Jesus and His disciples were full of the Holy Spirit and led by Him, and it is the Holy Spirit who continues to set up stumbling blocks for people. He still moves in unlikely people and also often causes strange manifestations, which we will now investigate further.

Offensive Manifestations

At the very first outpouring of the Holy Spirit, He came with power that attracted a crowd, but He also engineered some offensive manifestations. As mentioned previously, the Holy Spirit overwhelmed the disciples, and people judged them to be drunk. They made fun of them and said, "They have had too much wine" (Acts 2:13). This was humbling to the disciples who immediately had to defend themselves and argue their case. They declared, "These people are not drunk, as you suppose. It's only nine in the morning!" (Acts 2:15). If the crowd accepted their explanation, they would be humbled as well because they would have to tolerate preachers who looked drunk.

The Bible does not spell out what caused the drunken appearance of the disciples, but they may have staggered around and slurred their words. They may have lost their balance and ended up on the floor. In other places in the Bible, there are accounts of people falling to the ground in the presence of God (see Dan. 8:17; 10:7-10,15-19; 1 Kings 8:10-11; John 18:5; Rev. 1:17), faces shining supernaturally (see Exod. 34:29-35; Acts 6:15), trances (see Acts 10:10; 2 Cor. 5:12-13), temporary blindness (see Acts 9:8-9) or numbness (see Luke 1:22), trumpet sounds (see Exod. 19:19), nature phenomena such as smoke and earthquakes (see 1 Kings 8:10-11; Matt. 27:51), and lightning and thunder (see Exod. 19:16-19). This is a long list, but it is not even complete and no clue seems to be given as to what can be expected.

We know from church history that these manifestations have not always been welcome among Christians. Entire movements have been judged and rejected on the basis of strange commotions. Nevertheless,

God confronts us with them and sets them up in all of their awkwardness and offensiveness. One pastor reports:

> ...there were some instances of persons lying in a sort of trance...It was a very frequent thing to see outcries, faintings, convulsions, and such like, both with distress, and also admiration and joy....."[1]

In my own limited experience, I would say that quieter manifestations such as tears of repentance and silent joy are often acceptable. However, not many churches would be able to accommodate outcries and convulsions. Strong feelings and loud noises make many of us nervous. Even so, is this God trying to offend us and upsetting our notions of religion and respectability? At the very first outpouring of the Holy Spirit, He filled the house with a sound like the blowing of a violent wind. This was unexpected and not foretold in the Scriptures; nevertheless, it happened by God's design.

Offensive Operations

The Holy Spirit is not shy in causing strange manifestations, and He is also not shy in manifesting further strangeness through the way He operates in us and through us. When Moses and the people of Israel were wedged between the hostile Egyptian army and the Red Sea, they needed help from God to stay alive. It was then that God told Moses, "Raise your staff and stretch out your hand over the sea to divide the water so that the Israelites can go through the sea on dry ground" (Exod. 14:16). How foolish this must have felt to Moses! In full view of all the people, he was asked to do the impossible by absurdly raising a stick over the water and stretching out his hand. Who had ever heard that this would achieve anything? What if nothing had happened?

The Spirit's strange operations were also a challenge to Jesus. At one time, He was prompted to heal a blind man with bizarre medicine: "He spit on the ground, made some mud with the saliva, and put it on the man's eyes" (John 9:6). This seemed to be a gross method of healing. At other times, the healings seemed to come with more dignity and Jesus healed people by the power of His word or touch, but not in this instance. He had to accept the Spirit's strange leadings and submit absolutely. The Son of God had to mix His spit with dirt and smear the concoction into a blind man's eyes. The question is whether modern Christians would take offense at such healings today and shut down this kind of ministry.

Many a time in the past, the prophets of God were asked not only to speak His word but also release the Spirit's power through unusual and even "kooky" behavior. Ezekiel shaved his head and beard; then beat, burned, and scattered his hair (see Ezek. 5:1-12). Isaiah went naked for three years (see Isa. 20). Jeremiah carried a wooden yoke on his neck (see Jer. 27:1-28); he tied a stone to a scroll of prophetic words and threw it into the Euphrates River (see Jer. 51:62-64). Hosea married a prostitute (see Hosea 1:1-11). Ahijah tore the king's new garment into twelve pieces (see 1 Kings 11:30-40), and Elisha insisted on striking the ground with arrows for victory over Israel's enemies (see 2 Kings 13:14-18).

What would we make of this today? It is easy to take offense at such actions and it is easy to understand why God's people would not want to be associated with anything as weird as walking around naked and striking the ground with arrows. Yet, the Spirit offends us on purpose because He desires to shame the wisdom of the wise. Therefore, we better rethink our attitude and maybe the church can recognize that even the foundational blessings of baptism and Holy Communion share in the same "kooky" behavior because, from a rational point of view, what can a bath in water achieve for salvation and how can a meal of bread and wine communicate Jesus' forgiveness?

Offensive Miracles

People take offense at the Holy Spirit because sometimes He is causing strange manifestations and is working through strange means. This is regrettable, but there is more. In my own experience, I have also found that people get upset with the kind of miracles that the Holy Spirit works among His people. Ever since the last Sunday of 2009, God has made gold dust appear on our church attendants and also manifested the same miracle during the week. Even many of my friends have remained indifferent to this unexpected display of love from God. One dear colleague assured me of his support but told me, "I know that you are into this kind of thing, but I am not." It made no difference to him and others that our congregation never petitioned God for the specific miracle of gold dust. God did this of His own accord, and we could only respond with either thanksgiving or rejection.

At one of our prayer meetings, I showed a video of a healing evangelist who prayed for church leaders to begin operating in the supernatural. He also mentioned gold dust and other miracles. In the light of our own experience, I was excited about the ministry; but an older church member who had come to us from a Pentecostal background, stood up and spoke with anger, "This is fluff. This is not a real revival. God wants to do so much more. Gold dust is nothing." I still remember how surprised I was. The person had no problems accepting miracles, but refused to embrace this particular miracle. She ended up handing out literature suggesting that this kind of miracle could be of demonic origin.

However, God is God and we are not. We were so hungry for God to confirm His word with signs and wonders. How could we complain about the kind of miracle He chose to give us first? In my view, God was extremely gentle with us because He did not require us to embrace anything that was wild. Gold dust was not making us fall down. It had no odor. It stained no clothes. It was not noisy. It just made us look beautiful, as the bride of Christ. In a gentle way, God was saying to us, "I love you." Even unexperienced Christians, newcomers, and Lutherans should be able to handle this experience.

The Holy Spirit has a habit of offending people, and sometimes it does not take much for people to take offense. I was very surprised at how people could believe the miracles in the Bible yet became upset with miracles today. One day I talked to an older colleague after a prayer meeting, and I shared with him my frustration over the quenching of the Spirit. He told me that he had been to meetings in the 1970s where God would supernaturally provide gold fillings for teeth, then he asked, "Why would God do that?" He did not understand; therefore, he pulled back from these kinds of miracles. Why? The conversation with him did not ease my frustration.

Anyone with an aching tooth would probably have appreciated a gold filling from God rather than the dentist. It was a token of love from God that caused no pain and cost no money. Yet, people were and are offended. I was at a conference where an older woman shared how God made manna appear in her husband's Bible. It appeared on the page with the reference to the "hidden manna" for those who overcome (see Rev. 2:17) and the manna kept appearing on the same Bible page throughout his life. He and his wife were Lutherans, but their church community could not handle the miracle—even though it replicated one from the Bible. Thus they were expelled from the congregation.

After hearing this testimony, I have at times asked for the same miracle; and during the worship service, I have opened my Bible to Revelation 2:17—but I am still waiting for this specific miracle. This one has a precedent in the Bible, and it would be wonderful to taste what the people of Israel tasted for forty years in the wilderness. Does it really taste like honey wafers? (See Exodus 16:31.) However, not all miracles require a Bible precedent; God is creative and supplies miracles in such abundance that the Bible cannot contain them all (see John 21:25). Consequently, our church has also been rejoicing over oil manifesting on the palm of people's hands; and we believe others when they talk about supernatural rain inside their worship building, angel feathers, and gem stones in their midst. As a pastor, I can only encourage everyone not to take offense but rather allow God to be God. He has made His intentions clear in the Bible:

> *Jesus did many other miraculous signs in the presence of his disciples, which are not recorded in this book. But these are written that you may believe that Jesus is the Christ, the Son of God, and that by believing you may have life in his name* (John 20:30-32 NIV 1984).

> *Believe me when I say that I am in the Father and the Father is in me; or at least believe on the evidence of the miracles themselves. I tell you the truth, anyone who has faith in me will do what I have been doing. He will do even greater things than these, because I am going to the Father* (John 14:11-12 NIV 1984).

Offensive Diversity

The Holy Spirit offends human wisdom with strange manifestations, operations, and miracles, but there is still more. There is also the offense of unexpected diversity. For instance, Billy Graham and Benny

Hinn have both been bearing fruit as evangelists at the same time, but only the latter has moved more intentionally in the power for healing miracles. Rick Warren and Gene Edwards have been outstanding church builders in the United States, but only the former has planted a megachurch while the latter has set in motion a house church movement. All of these people have been blessed by God, but their diversity has often been confusing for the Christian church and people have taken sides rather than embrace the diversity.

This kind of confusion has been with the church from the beginning. When the apostle Paul sought to unite divided church camps in Corinth, he argued that it was not of the Spirit to play one minister against the other because they were serving the same God and accomplishing different assignments (see 1 Cor. 3:1-10). In more general terms, the apostle Paul explained to the people in Corinth that the Holy Spirit is always expressing Himself in diversity, but it is still the same Holy Spirit who works through people:

> *There are different kinds of gifts, but the same Spirit distributes them. There are different kinds of service, but the same Lord. There are different kinds of working, but in all of them and in everyone it is the same God at work* (1 Corinthians 12:4-6).

Jesus Himself began His work in the midst of the greatest confusion. He had a forerunner in the person of John the Baptist and embraced his work so that for a time they were both baptizing people in close proximity to each other:

> *After this, Jesus and his disciples went out into the Judean countryside, where he spent some time with them, and baptized. Now John also was baptizing at Aenon near Salim, because there was plenty of water, and people were coming and being baptized* (John 3:22-23; see also John 4:1-2).

It looked like people had to make a choice between John and Jesus. According to the Bible, both men were faithful servants of God, but they were as different from each other as chalk and cheese. The Holy Spirit moved in both, but in confounding diversity.

If John had nursed the hope that the coming Christ would be a more powerful version of himself, he would have been bitterly disappointed. His own parents were old and respectable descendants of priests, and John was their miracle baby God granted them past child-bearing age—everyone rejoiced in his birth (see Luke 1:5-25,57-66). However, Jesus' parents were young and poor, and the Holy Spirit caused his mother's pregnancy before marriage so that the miracle baby Jesus was born out of wedlock, away from home and in disgrace (see Matt. 1:18-25).

While John was full of the Holy Spirit from birth, with the stipulation never to consume alcohol (see Luke 1:15), Jesus turned water into wine as the very first miracle He performed in the power of the Holy Spirit (see John 2:1-11) and He was known to drink wine Himself (see Luke 7:34). In contrast to Jesus, John never performed a single miracle in his work of preaching repentance to God's people; but Jesus not only performed many of them, He relied on them for the confirmation of His preaching (see John 10:25-26,32,38). Contrary to John's own experience, God used miracles to certify the calling and identity of Jesus:

> *…Jesus…was a man accredited by God to you by miracles, wonders and signs, which God did among you through him…* (Acts 2:22).

John and his disciples were fasting, but Jesus and His disciples were not (see Matt. 9:14-15). It must have been very confusing to see these two men, John and Jesus, work side by side. Both were full of the Spirit and faithful to their calling. Both preached, "Repent for the kingdom of heaven has come near" (Matt. 3:2; 4:17). Both had a national ministry and raised high hopes in their followers; but, in many respects, they were different from each other and represented different seasons in God's work. Jesus would not only baptize with water but also the Holy Spirit.

Throughout church history, God has been working with confounding diversity. It has not always been easy to embrace all the moves and seasons in God because many a time new seasons come with new and unexpected modes of operation and manifestations. We all need humility in the face of God who is determined to shame our wisdom and nullify our human expertise. On purpose, the Holy Spirit keeps setting up stumbling blocks for proud people through strange manifestations, operations, miracles, and also unexpected diversity.

Jeopardizing His Own Work

As a pastor, I have often wondered why God was not more support-ive of my call. While I was trying to keep the peace and avoid conflict, He was upsetting our good church members with divine intent. What was I to do? This was not helping me and undermined God's own reputation. Why would He attach a stigma to His work? Why would God jeopardize His own plans of reaching a lost world? If He wants people to be saved, why does He offend them? If He wants the church to support His mission, why make us struggle with discernment?

Evangelist Charles Finney came to a place where he worked with the Presbyterian minister for the revival of the village, which almost imme-diately commenced. A few years earlier, there had already been a revival in that village under the labors of the Methodists. It had been attended with a good deal of excitement and many cases occurred of what the Methodists referred to as "falling under the power of God." This the Presbyterians had resisted; and in consequence, a bad state of feeling had existed between the Methodists and the Presbyterians; the Methodists accusing the Presbyterians of having opposed the revival among them because of these cases of falling under the power of God.

One day as Finney was preaching, he observed a man falling from his seat near the door. He was satisfied that it was a genuine case of "falling under the power of God," but he feared that it might again divide and alienate the faithful and thus stop the revival. However, the person who had fallen to the floor was one of the principal members of the Presbyterian church. And during the entire revival, whenever any-one was falling under the power of God, it was always a Presbyterian—not one Methodist.[2]

Maybe this was God's sense of humor. The two Christian commu-nities repented of their divisions, and the revival continued. Yet can we see what risk God seemed to take in making another person fall under His power? Why not let him be decently converted sitting on a chair? Why cause a commotion and offend good church people?

What is further puzzling is the unimportant nature of the offending manifestation. Falling from his chair had nothing to do with the salva-tion of the man in Finney's worship service. Manifestations like fluttering eyelids, tingling skin, or jerking are not essential and are not promised to us in the Bible. Unless a person repents of his sins and puts his faith in Jesus Christ, any reaction of the body to the supernatural power of God is of no avail. It is only faith that gains friendship with God.

God does seem to jeopardize His own work. On the one hand, He has come to seek and save the lost; but on the other hand, He confuses them with strange methods and manifestations. From a human perspective, we may not appreciate this inherent contradiction, but the perspective changes as we submit to God's sovereignty with supernatural joy. This is what happened to Jesus:

> *At that time Jesus, full of joy through the Holy Spirit, said, "I praise you, Father, Lord of heaven and earth, because you have hidden these things from the wise and learned, and revealed them to little children. Yes, Father, for this is what you were pleased to do"* (Luke 10:21).

Handling Manifestations

For all of their divine origin and intent, the Spirit's strange manifestations, operations, miracles, and unexpected diversity remain a challenge for people in church leadership. Everyone might agree that it would not be wise to suppress genuine responses to the Holy Spirit, such as intense conviction and supreme joy in the individual. However, not all manifestations are caused by the Holy Spirit. There are also demonic counterfeits that look the same because "Satan himself masquerades as an angel of light" (2 Cor. 11:14).

Furthermore, there is the less serious but more frequent hazard of immature people faking the manifestations. Since outcomes like falling to the ground or jerking are noticed by others and confirm the operations of the Spirit, immature people often want this kind of recognition and, on occasion, simply fake the manifestations. In most cases, this is not hard for them because anyone can fall to the ground or jerk their body. Thus, they appear spiritual.

In 2008, God TV broadcasted a prominent outpouring of the Holy Spirit in the United States for a number of months. Soon after, there were Christians who exhibited the same kind of spiritual "head shaking" as the key leader of the outpouring. Was this physical manifestation genuine, or did it come with watching too much television?

Suspicions arise when the manifestation remains clearly under the control of the person who can decide when to switch it on and when to turn it off.

Another version of faking manifestations is the "courtesy drop." Some Christians want to assure those who pray and lay hands on others that the Spirit is working through them. They especially want to encourage guest preachers; therefore, they respond to their ministry by politely falling to the floor. This does not hurt them, but lessens the anxiety of the visiting pastor. When I first heard about the "courtesy drop," I thought it was funny. First people tend to get upset by a manifestation, and then it is so much in demand that people fake it as an expression of courtesy.

Therefore, the challenge remains. How can a church community find their way through the strangeness of manifestations, demonic counterfeits and fakes? The common temptation is probably to sort out the excesses too soon. Yet Jesus told a parable where He clearly admonished His disciples not to separate the weeds from the wheat before harvest time because "while you are pulling the weeds, you may uproot the wheat with them" (Matt. 13:29).

I remember one instance when a young man was making strange bopping actions while groaning loudly. After a while, my impression was that he was simply drawing attention to himself and prolonging the public ministry. However, later I was humbled when I listened to his testimony. He explained that, during this time of strange manifestations, God was healing him of the sexual abuse he had suffered as a young boy. Thus, as uncomfortable as it may often be, we need to refrain from rushing in and sorting out the genuine manifestations from the fakes because we cannot always tell them apart before the ministry has finished.

At the same time, we are not to be completely passive. The Bible admonishes us to let all things be done, but they are to be done "in a fitting and orderly way" (1 Cor. 14:40). On the basis of Matthew 7:20 ("by their fruit you will recognize them"), Pastor Jonathan Edwards devised five diagnostic questions that may be used to test spiritual manifestations:

1. Does it bring honor to the person of Jesus Christ?

2. Does it produce a greater hatred of sin and a greater love for righteousness?

3. Does it produce a greater regard for Scripture?

4. Does it lead people into truth?

5. Does it produce a greater love for God and people?[3]

These five diagnostic questions help us to cut through the distractions and fakes and focus on what the Holy Spirit first and foremost wants to do. According to Jesus, He intends to bring glory to Him (see John 16:14).

In any church meeting, it may be further helpful to remind people that manifestations are not the goal of the service and ministry. We all want an encounter with God, but this can happen without any effects on our bodies. For instance, Jesus said that He lived on every word that came out of the mouth of His Father (see Matt. 4:4), and these words can be heard without falling off a chair. Most of all, we need love to overcome the offense and divisiveness of manifestations. Therefore, let us encourage each other with humility.

Receiving by Foolishness

When the Holy Spirit increased His intensity in our church, the most dominant manifestation was the falling down under the power of the Spirit. This was a surprise because it happened without warning. I was catching our members on their way down, but had never previously been in a worship service where anything like this had happened. My immediate reaction was the personal resolve that losing one's balance was not necessary for receiving from God. Thus, I let the guest preacher lay hands on me and pray, but made sure that I had my feet firmly planted on the floor in a defensive stance. In my case, God would have to be decisive and push me over before I would go down.

This was fine. However, five years later, God taught me a lesson. I was at a conference where the main speaker taught on spiritual impartation and then invited pastors to receive the same through the laying on of hands and prayer. As I recollect, I was the first one lining up in front of the platform; I was there before the pastors were even called. The worship band kept playing and somehow, from deep within me, I began shouting the name of Jesus in desperation. I did not even know how desperate I was.

Then, it was my turn to be prayed for, and I began to lose my balance. I thought that this may have been caused by the jam-packed prayer line and quickly wanted to take a step back to prevent my body from falling. However, my right leg was stuck. It felt as if the person next to me tripped me. I could not help but fall backward, and I was disappointed. I thought, *God, this is not You. Someone will catch me but this is not the impartation.*

Then the Spirit came upon me in power on the way down to the floor. For a long time, I was weeping and also convulsing. God spoke to me and shared His heart about our congregation and denomination. This was a precious time. Back at home, I watched the conference videos and wanted to identify the person who tripped me at the moment of receiving prayer. There was no one close enough to interfere with my stance. Could it be that God had commissioned an angel to trip me and send this stubborn German to the floor? Could it be that God had used some special measures to make me vulnerable enough so that I could receive from Him?

As I could not correct my footing and was falling down, I was completely helpless in the air; and for the duration of the fall, I had to surrender all control. This was precisely the moment in time that God used for His purposes, and ever since I learned to be light on my feet. As soon as I feel the Holy Spirit moving on me, I now let go of control and welcome the fall, because many times the Spirit expands His ministry while I am on the floor.

This has been my experience—but not mine alone. In fact, as a pastor I encounter many people in the prayer line who are sharing my initial resistance to falling down. No one is keen to be vulnerable and lose control of the body. Who knows whether the person behind me will catch me? Then there is the "foolish" aspect of a well-dressed church person ending up on the floor. Yet those who choose to embrace the foolishness often receive for the first time according to the deep wisdom of the Bible, which explains that "God chose the foolish things of the world to shame the wise" (1 Cor. 1:27). God wants "to nullify the things that are" (1 Cor. 1:28), and this includes our sense of control and propriety.

One time, I was preaching in an Anglican church and, after the sermon, a long-time church member said to me, "As I was listening to you, I realized that I have no personal relationship with God. I used to have one; but then there was so much grief in my life that I retreated from God." I encouraged her to speak out a prayer of repentance and then proceeded to pray for her with the laying on of hands. After a while, she became wobbly on her feet, and I could see that she did not know what was happening. I asked her how she felt and she responded, "My heart is getting warm and filled with love." She had an encounter with God and she knew that her relationship with God was being renewed. She was happy.

However, she did not understand what was happening to her legs. I tried to explain that this was also the Holy Spirit moving on her, but she did not know what to do and fought the sensation. This made further prayer ministry more difficult because she no longer submitted control to God. I quickly asked an assistant to bring a chair so that she could relax sitting down and not worry about her balance. However, it was too late. She could not get back to a surrendered state in this prayer session. This was okay because she had made a fresh beginning with God, and God would always be with her, but it showed me again the importance of embracing the foolishness of falling down. Whatever God wants to do, we let him do it.

My eldest daughter, Dominique, confirmed this observation. After a day of teaching on the Spirit in our church, she was also in the prayer line, and I prayed for her. She was immediately impacted by the prayer, and I sensed the Spirit flowing into her. Her body began to drift and lean backward, but then she stepped in, cut off the flow and stopped the movement. She felt uncomfortable falling backward in the church. I explained to her that she was quenching the Spirit in her resistance and proceeded to pray for her again, but she could not overcome the hurdle of feeling awkward about falling down.

Three days later, we had a prayer time in our own living room and this time she was determined to let go of control. She wanted to be absolutely surrendered to God and, within a few seconds, down she went under the power of the Spirit. This made her rather joyful. She felt that she had achieved something in embracing God's kind of foolishness in order to receive from Him.

May every Christian experience this kind of breakthrough and then be prepared for more because God remains creative in confronting us with foolishness. Later we will spend some time on the spiritual gift of speaking in tongues, which also appears foolish to some because the mind cannot comprehend the "babble" coming from the mouth. Thus, many Christians want to be filled with the Spirit, but insist that this needs to happen without receiving the gift of tongues. They do not want to embrace this kind of weirdness. Yet, it is not wise to be in control and dictate the terms when God wants "to nullify the things that are" (1 Cor. 1:28).

God often, by design and on purpose, confronts us with foolishness to shame our notions of pride and respectability. Thus it seems good advice to prepare ourselves for the foolishness that may come our way, and then also go on the offensive. If we know that God wants to shame the wise, why would we not intentionally do something humbling and foolish in our public worship services? We could actively pursue God by surrendering our pride to Him. For many Lutherans, this is quite easy and requires no effort or expense. They could simply raise their hands in worship. This form of worship is common in the Bible, but not in traditional mainline worship services. When people do it for the first time, they feel quite self-conscious and embarrassed, but this kind of folly actively invites and surrenders to God whose "foolishness…is wiser than human wisdom" and whose "weakness…is stronger than human strength" (1 Cor. 1:25).

ENDNOTES

1. Jonathan Edwards, quoted in *The Toronto Blessing* by Dave Roberts (Eastbourne, England: Kingsway Publishing, 1994), 131-132.

2. Charles Finney, *Original Memoirs of Charles G. Finney* (Grand Rapids, MI: Zondervan, 2002), 108.

3. Jonathan Edwards, referenced (not quoted) in *Growing in the Prophetic* by Mike Bickle with Michael Sullivant (Orlando, FL: Creation House, 1996), 207.

Chapter 6

The Battle Is On

THE HOLY SPIRIT AND SPIRITUAL WARFARE

Not that many years ago, New Testament scholar Rudolph Bult-mann impacted the Christian world with these words:

> It is impossible to use electric light and the wireless and to avail ourselves of modern medical and surgical discoveries, and at the same time believe in the New Testament world of spirits and miracles…. [This is] unintelligible and unacceptable to the modern world.
>
> Human knowledge and mastery of the world have advanced to such an extent through science and technology that it is no longer possible for anyone seriously to hold the New Testament view of the world—in fact, there is no one who does…Now that the forces and the laws of nature have been discovered, we can no longer believe in spirits, whether good or bad.[1]

At the time, these words seemed to be the compelling truth even for many Christians. I still remember how my pastor, who taught me religion in high school, seemed to have no answers against these judgments but tried nevertheless to cling to one last supernatural hope, which was the resurrection from the dead of Jesus Christ and eternal life for all those who put their faith in Him. Back then, it seemed as if any respectable person of intelligence must agree with the view that modern science ruled out any place for the supernatural in this world.

All the same, even if it sounds primitive and behind the times, we cannot tone down the supernatural elements of the Christian faith because a church without the supernatural is a church without God and without the power of the Holy Spirit operating in it. In such a church you cannot survive because you become defenseless against the powers of darkness that keep operating despite electric light and the wireless.

Charged for Battle

A few years ago, a book like this one would have been challenging to me because it would have confronted me with the active side of the Holy Spirit who is still causing words of prophecy, bold preaching, speaking in tongues, manifestations such as people falling to the ground, laughing, shaking, and being filled with the love of God. It would not have been easy for me to reacquaint myself with these Bible realities in modern times, and many of the testimonies would have sounded a little spooky to me. Yet, in this chapter, the challenge goes even further. The Holy Spirit is not the only supernatural persona among us. He comes upon Christians, charges them with power, and then, without fail, leads them into battle with the unholy spirits of satan.

When Jesus was about thirty years old, He was praying and, "heaven was opened and the Holy Spirit descended on him in bodily form like a dove" (Luke 3:21-22). Immediately after the Spirit had descended on Him, the battle was on. "Jesus, full of the Spirit…was led by the Spirit into the wilderness, where for forty days he was tempted by the devil" (Luke 4:1-2). Tempted but not overcome, Jesus announced His new mission with these words:

> *The Spirit of the Lord is* [now] *upon me…to proclaim freedom for the prisoners…to set the oppressed free…* (Luke 4:18-19).

This He proceeded to accomplish by preaching the kingdom of God and confronting the demons of satan with power. I quote from the same Bible chapter that announced Jesus' mission:

> *Then he…began to teach the people. They were amazed…because his message had authority. …an evil spirit…cried out at the top of his voice, "Ha! What do you want with us, Jesus of Nazareth? Have you come to destroy us?" …"Be quiet!" Jesus said sternly. "Come out of him!" …All the people were amazed and said to each other, "What is this teaching? With authority and power he*

gives orders to evil spirits and they come out!" ...When the sun was setting, the people brought to Jesus all who had various kinds of sickness, and laying his hands on each one, he healed them. Moreover, demons came out of many people, shouting, "You are the Son of God!"... (Luke 4:31-44 NIV 1984)

His disciples later summarized this period of Jesus' ministry by saying, "God anointed Jesus of Nazareth with the Holy Spirit and power...he went around doing good and healing all who were under the power of the devil..." (Acts 10:38). Thus, when the Spirit had come upon Jesus with power, He began to confront the dominion of satan and heal all those under the power of satan.

This continued until the climax of the cross where satan struck back with force. Toward the end, "Satan entered Judas" (Luke 22:3), a disciple from Jesus' inner circle, who subsequently betrayed Jesus and began an evil chain of events whereby Jesus was arrested, spat upon, disowned, mocked, insulted, sneered at, tortured, and finally killed by having His body pinned to a cross with nails. At that time, satan seemed to have his way and finally triumph. Even Jesus conceded this season to satan and said, "...this is your hour—when darkness reigns" (Luke 22:53).

Yet, the confrontation took a decisive turn when Jesus' death was not satan's final victory but his ultimate defeat. Jesus' death on the cross defeated satan in a battle of cosmic proportions because it turned out to be the redeeming sacrifice for all sinners who could rightly be accused by satan. Jesus' death surprised satan with sudden defeat by removing all grounds for accusations and guilt. From now on, sinful humans would go free from his clutches because the innocent blood of Jesus, His amazing sacrifice, paid the price for our iniquity and thus contains the power to wash away all of our sins.

The Bible declares:

having disarmed the powers and authorities [of Satan], *he made a public spectacle of them, triumphing over them by the cross* (Colossians 2:15).

...The reason the Son of God appeared was to destroy the devil's work (1 John 3:8).

What is more, Jesus made this victory complete and beyond any doubt when He rose from the grave after three days. It was then that death had been "swallowed up in victory" (1 Cor. 15:54).

Jesus' entire ministry was about the supernatural contest between God and satan—who was not equal to God but was His main adversary. Hence, these Scripture references are only a small selection of many passages dealing with this dominant theme. This is not in dispute among Christians; but for all practical purposes, the whole subject matter of any supernatural contest between God and satan did not seem to have any relevance in my own life. For years, I managed to avoid preaching on demons and satan because, in our modern times, we did not seem to be dealing with this kind of spiritual warfare. At least, I had never knowingly encountered a demon.

Yet the Bible clearly teaches that satan retains much power even now and will only be completely destroyed at the end of time when Jesus returns to earth in glory:

> *The great dragon was hurled down—that ancient serpent called the devil, or Satan, who leads the whole world astray. ...He is filled with fury, because he knows that his time is short. ...* [He] *went off to wage war against...those who keep God's commands and hold fast their testimony about Jesus* (Revelation 12:9-17).

> *And the devil, who deceived them, was thrown into the lake of burning sulphur...They will be tormented day and night for ever and ever* (Revelation 20:10).

For this reason, Jesus insisted that His disciples needed the power of the Spirit to be effective in mission. With relentless energy, their mission would be opposed by satan and his minions. Thus, when Jesus first taught His disciples that repentance and forgiveness of sins would be preached in His name, He immediately clarified that a perfect understanding of this truth and their commissioning by Him would not be enough to get the job done. They needed more of the Holy Spirit; therefore, He commanded them to wait in their current location until they had been "clothed with power from on high" (Luke 24:49).

When this happened and the Holy Spirit had come on them, the disciples soon found themselves in a permanent battle with the forces of evil; and according to the Bible, the same spiritual conflict with satan and his demons remains an ongoing reality for all Christians:

> *For our struggle is not against flesh and blood, but against the rulers, against the authorities, against the powers of this dark world and against the spiritual forces of evil in the heavenly realms* (Ephesians 6:12).

> *The god of this age* [Satan] *has blinded the minds of unbelievers, so that they cannot see the light of the gospel that displays the glory of Christ, who is the image of God* (2 Corinthians 4:4).

> *...I am sending you to them to open their eyes and turn them from darkness to light, and from the power of Satan to God, so that they may receive forgiveness of sins and a place among those who are sanctified by faith in me* (Acts 26:17-18).

> *As for you, you were dead in your transgressions and sins, in which you used to live when you followed the ways of this world and of the ruler of the kingdom of the air, the spirit who is now at work in those who are disobedient* (Ephesians 2:1-2).

> *And do not give the devil a foothold* (Ephesians 4:27).

Martin Luther, like many other church fathers, agreed with the Scriptures and wrote the following in his basic instructions to clergy:

> This is why Christians have to be armed and expect every day to face constant attacks…He is the kind of enemy who never gives up or gets tired. When one temptation stops, new ones take its place. …In Greek this phrase ["deliver us from evil" which is the last petition of the Lord's Prayer] reads: "Save (or protect) us from the Evil One (or the Wicked One)." *This petition seems to refer to the devil, as if to compress everything into the one idea that the sum total of all our prayer should be aimed at this main enemy of ours* [emphasis added] …this petition also includes all the evil that can happen to us under the devil's rule: poverty, disgrace, death…all the… heartache which never ends here in the world. Because the devil is not only a liar but also a murderer, he never stops trying to kill us, and takes his anger out on us by doing what he can to get us hurt in accidents, and to do us physical harm. This is how he manages to break many a person's neck

and to drive others insane. Some he drowns, and many he pushes into suicide and many other terrible evils....[2]

As much as Lutherans appreciate the reformer Martin Luther, his core awareness of the evil one is no longer familiar to all church members. Yet, his insights are from the Bible and he experienced the reality of his teaching. As soon as someone is filled and charged with the Holy Spirit, he is ready and released to do mission work, which entails a battle with the unholy spirits of satan.

The Immediate Fight-Back

In 2003, God surprised us in a worship service with the guest preacher Gemechis Desta Buba, a Lutheran pastor from Ethiopia. Without anyone explaining anything to me, I recognized that this worship service was different from any other that I had attended. The atmosphere was rich with the presence of God. It was almost tangible and it had consequences.

One of our long-term church members was sitting in a pew, and he was not happy. Not only had his wife put pressure on him to attend the service, he also felt something stirring inside of him, besides the anger. A demon was manifesting. This greatly upset him. He was not at all comfortable with manifestations of the Holy Spirit and tried to keep Him at arm's length, but now an unholy spirit intimidated him by taking control with bouts of rage and thoughts of suicide. He knew that he was not his usual self and was frightened to have a demon in him. After a few days, aided by prophetic dreams and much prayer, he again experienced freedom.

After this whole episode, I wondered how I should make sense of what had happened. This demon must have been in my friend and church member for a long time and seemed to be linked to a family history of Freemasonry. Why did he not manifest earlier? I came to understand that the unusual intensity of God's presence in the service forced the demon to "blow his cover."

Usually, unclean spirits prefer to remain hidden in people so that they are not at risk of being confronted. This is in accordance with satan's normal strategy of blinding the minds of sinful people. Satan does not want them to identify the sins that allow him to gain footholds in their lives (see 2 Cor. 4:4; 11:14-15; Heb. 3:13). However, no demon can endure an intensified invasion of God's holy presence. Holy power makes the demon extremely uncomfortable, and he exposes himself as a result in order to make a last-ditch effort of resisting expulsion. In desperation, he may try to intimidate the human host and withstand the authority of Jesus' name, but his uncovering is already a sign of weakness and promises imminent victory.

Jesus' own ministry was marked by such encounters where demons reacted to His presence and authority by crying out and manifesting in people. For instance, the Bible records:

> *The people were amazed by his teaching, for he was teaching them with authority, not like the legal experts. Suddenly, there in the synagogue, a person with an evil spirit screamed, "What have you to do with us, Jesus of Nazareth? Have you come to destroy us? I know who you are. You are the holy one from God"* (Mark 1:22-24 Common English Bible).

> *At sunset, the people brought to Jesus all who had various kinds of sickness, and laying his hands on each one, he healed them. Moreover, demons came out of many people, shouting, "You are the Son of God!"…* (Luke 4:40-41)

The more I began to understand this dynamic, the more I began to get upset. At the service with Pastor Gemechis, the holiness of God confronted and forced the demon in our church member to "blow his cover." Why had this not happened earlier? For years, this person had been attending our weekly worship services. Why had this demon been comfortable sleeping through every service I was leading? This challenged me because I realized that somehow I was lacking spiritual authority and power, and a new hunger began rising within me. I wanted a stronger ministry that would upset the demonic strongholds.

In one Bible passage, an evil spirit said to some men, "Jesus I know, and Paul I know about, but who are you?" (Acts 19:15)? This evil spirit had never himself encountered Paul but knew his name and stature. I thought that it would be great if one day the demons would also know my name and respect the authority that I was wielding as a servant of Jesus; because at the moment of Pastor Gemechis' visit, they were still asking of me, "But who are you?"

Over the years, God gave me the desires of my heart and demons would manifest in response to my preaching and prayer ministry. God granted me a greater measure of power so that demons would even cause polite church people to stand up and speak out in opposition to the preaching—especially when I would proclaim Jesus' victory over satan.

Sometimes the demons would manifest without much preparation; but at other times, the demons would respond to a process of growing closer to Jesus. On one occasion, we had invited a family for dinner; as the mother was walking by me, I had the sudden knowledge of a demon inside her. I was not prepared for this kind of revelation because it was a social engagement, and I had no previous experience with such prophetic communication (see 1 Cor. 12:8). Yet, the revelation would prove to be correct.

Not much later, this woman came to us for counseling and began dealing with her past life and sins. God challenged her to give up control to Him. When she expressed her fears about trusting God, I encouraged her to ask God for a sign, which soon came in the form of dream. She dreamt that she was falling to her death from a high building, but at the last moment, was rescued by Jesus. Slowly, she edged closer to Jesus with the result of new and strange experiences at worship.

All of a sudden, the name of Jesus became intolerable to her in church. Whenever the name of Jesus was mentioned in singing, praying, and preaching, she would fly into a kind of rage that made her want to run out of the worship building. She felt embarrassed, but these are classic symptoms of an unclean spirit finally coming to the surface and making a last-ditch attempt to resist the power of Jesus and expulsion. There were also strong urges toward suicide and literal darkness clouding up her vision. She came to understand what was happening to her, but so far she has not been set free. Instead of engaging in the battle and achieving victory through Jesus, she turned away from the faith because she reasoned that less involvement with Jesus would quiet the demon again. It did not.

Not every person will need to battle a demon, but the general principle holds true for all Christians. As soon as we grow closer to Jesus, we will discover that the powers of darkness do not cede ground without fighting back. Seek more of the Holy Spirit, commit to holiness, or fall more in love with God and you will experience resistance in some form of spiritual oppression. For instance, there may be a new wave of temptations or circumstances that conspire against your peace in God.

A preacher shared this common observation: "People have been in meetings where the glory of God has fallen, where the fingerprints of God have been upon everything, and where fortifications have been made in the body. The next morning the power of Satan attacked them."[3]

The Bible also confirms the common fight-back attempts of the enemy against any advances of God's kingdom. As mentioned earlier, Jesus Himself experienced the baptism with the Spirit and at once found Himself in a battle against satan. Satan immediately challenged the confirmation of Jesus' sonship, which He had received at His Spirit baptism. Whatever Jesus had gained at His Spirit baptism, satan immediately challenged in a battle experience of fasting and temptation in the wilderness (see Luke 3:21-22; 4:1-13).

Other outstanding examples of fight-back attempts are the experiences of Moses, Elijah, and David. It is satan's common and persistent strategy to challenge immediately any breakthrough in God's work. When Moses finally obeyed God in Egypt and confronted Pharaoh with the request of releasing the slaves from Israel, God's people, the aggressive fight-back consisted of increasing the labor of the slaves. Pharaoh reacted by commanding his slave drivers, "You are no longer to supply the people with straw for making bricks...but...don't reduce the quota. ...Make the work harder for the people so that they keep working and pay no attention to lies" (Exod. 5:7-9).

It took ten national plagues of judgment before Pharaoh finally gave in to God and let the people of Israel go from Egypt. Especially the last breakthrough was decisive. All of Egypt, including Pharaoh, was mourning the death of their firstborn sons. At last, the power of God proved to be too strong for Pharaoh and the Egyptians urged the Israelites to hurry and leave the country (see Exod. 12:31-33). The former slaves did not even have to go empty-handed but received silver and gold from the Egyptians so that "they plundered the Egyptians" (Exod. 12:36).

However, this last decisive breakthrough was still not the end of the enemy's fight-back attempts. The Israelites could have been forgiven for rejoicing and relaxing in their victory. They now enjoyed freedom and plenty of plunder. God had demonstrated His superior power by putting the firstborn sons of their enemies to death. There seemed nothing more to fear. The Egyptians were glad to see them go.

Only, the rejoicing was cut short again, and this time the fight-back not only threatened to worsen their condition but extinguish them. Pharaoh had changed his mind and decided to pursue the Israelites so they were trapped between his army and the Red Sea. In desperation, the Israelites cried out to Moses: "It would have been better for us to serve the Egyptians than to die in the desert!" (Exod. 14:12). However, God delivered them by dividing the water and granting them safe passage through the Red Sea. Moreover, He drowned the Egyptian army in the very same water as they followed the Israelites into the sea. Not one of them survived (see Exod. 14:21-28). After this victory, there would be no more fight-back attempts from the Egyptians, but it took a long time to defeat this enemy without the experience of constant repercussions.

The prophet Elijah opposed the idolatry of King Ahab and Jezebel, his wife, and also experienced persistent backlashes after stunning victories. As they were killing the Lord's servants, Elijah invited the whole nation to Mount Carmel for a showdown between him and four hundred and fifty prophets of Baal. They were to sacrifice a bull each and call on the name of their respective gods to light the fire of the sacrifice. Elijah taunted the prophets of Baal and mocked their prayers because there was no response.

Then, he drenched his bull with water, prayed, and the fire of the Lord fell and consumed not only the sacrifice but also the stones of the altar. King Ahab and the entire nation of Israel witnessed the superior power of the Lord and turned against idolatry and the prophets of Baal, whom Elijah killed with the sword. The crowning climax of the day came when, at the word of Elijah and his prayers, the three-year-long drought was broken and rain refreshed the land (see 1 Kings 18).

Elijah probably expected that this triumph was decisive enough to establish a lasting breakthrough whereby the idolatry of Ahab and

Jezebel was removed from the nation of Israel. He had won the power encounter on Mount Carmel. Four hundred and fifty prophets of Baal were dead. Before the King and the nation, God performed miracles and brought glory to Himself.

Yet, it was not enough. There would still be another fight-back attempt. Immediately, the King's wife, Jezebel, threatened Elijah with death so that "Elijah was afraid and ran for his life" (1 Kings 19:3). After all the intensity of Mount Carmel, the prophet crumbled under the renewed onslaught and wandered into the desert in despair. He wanted to die. Eventually, he was restored and lasting victory came in God's time, but his experience was not unusual. The enemy always attempts a fight-back after a spiritual breakthrough and the fight-back attempts are persistent even after spectacular victories. As Christians, we must expect and prepare for them.

It was the same for King David who had been contending hostile forces for years before he was crowned king. The triumph of his coronation was not the end of opposition. Another immediate fight-back occurred. Twice the full force of an enemy army challenged his new-found authority:

> *When the Philistines heard that David had been anointed king over Israel, they went up in full force to search for him, but David heard about it and went down to the stronghold. ... So David went to Baal Perazim, and there he defeated them. ...Once more the Philistines came up...David did as the Lord commanded him, and he struck down the Philistines all the way from Gibeon to Gezer* (2 Samuel 5:17-25).

The experience of David demonstrates again that spiritual breakthroughs are followed by the enemy's immediate attempt to recover lost ground. God had assigned kingship to David, but there was persistent opposition.

One last example may be Jesus' own experience of reaching amazing powers for healing, only to face inane inquisitions in response. Jesus no longer even touched the sick. The Spirit's presence on Jesus spilled over to His clothing so that any contact with the edge of His cloak accomplished perfect healing for the sick. Yet, the religious authorities were still not satisfied and tested the resolve of Jesus by confronting Him with queries about hand washing regulations rather than embracing His kingdom authority:

> *And when the men of that place recognized Jesus, they sent word to all the surrounding country. People brought all their sick to him and begged him to let the sick just touch the edge of his cloak, and all who touched it were healed. Then some Pharisees and teachers of the law came to Jesus from Jerusalem and asked, "Why do your disciples break the tradition of the elders? They don't wash their hands before they eat!"* (Matthew 14:35–15:2).

The Word as a Weapon

It is the common Christian experience that any advance in the kingdom of God through the Holy Spirit leads us into battle and makes us confront unholy spirits who are staging immediate fight-backs to win back lost territory. Yet God is promising us lasting victory. The battles must not frighten us. New ground will not always remain contested ground. However, there is the question about our weapons of warfare. How do we win the fight? This is a big topic, but my intention in this chapter is to present only a small survey and then concentrate on one feature of fighting only.

The most foundational activity and weapon in spiritual warfare is prayer, and it is exemplified in the picture of Moses whose arms needed to remain uplifted in prayer for victory over Israel's enemies: "As long as Moses held up his hands, the Israelites were winning, but whenever he lowered his hands, the Amalekites were winning" (Exod. 17:11).

The prayers for victory may simply consist of praise songs as in the following case:

> *...Jehoshaphat appointed men to sing to the Lord and to praise him for the splendour of his holiness as they went out at the head of the army, saying: 'Give thanks to the Lord, for his love endures forever.'* **As they began to sing and praise, the Lord set ambushes against the men of Ammon and Moab and Mount Seir** *who were invading Judah, and they were defeated* (2 Chronicles 20:21-22).

The Battle Is On

More weapons are: Jesus' name, His blood, and the testimony to the truth:

> *...Finally Paul became so annoyed that he turned around and said to the spirit, "In the name of Jesus Christ I command you to come out of her!" At that moment the spirit left her* (Acts 16:18).

> *They triumphed over him by the blood of the Lamb and by the word of their testimony...* (Revelation 12:11).

The Bible lists several more pieces in the Christian's armor for warfare:

> *Therefore put on the **full armor of God**, so that when the day of evil comes, you may be able to stand your ground, and after you have done everything, to stand. Stand firm then, with **the belt of truth** buckled around your waist, with **the breastplate of righteousness** in place, and with your feet fitted with **the readiness that comes from the gospel of peace**. In addition to all this, take up **the shield of faith**, with which you can extinguish all the flaming arrows of the evil one. Take **the helmet of salvation and the sword of the Spirit**, which is the word of God. And **pray in the Spirit on all occasions** with all kinds of prayers and requests. With this in mind, be alert and always keep on praying for all the Lord's people* (Ephesians 6:13-18).

In the midst of ongoing prayers, Christians depend on the defensive powers of the truth, righteousness, peace, and faith. However, there is also the offensive weapon of the word of God, which is nothing less than the "the sword of the Spirit."

I want to make a few more comments about the "sword of the Spirit." We need this weapon. Its importance cannot be overemphasized. The word of God and the accuracy of our understanding the word determine whether we win or lose against the powers of darkness. Satan can only gain a foothold in people and make them sin if they believe a lie. The battle for sin always begins in the mind because it is always the sowing of a sinful thought that reaps a sinful action. Thus, Neil Anderson emphasized in his spiritual warfare manual that "Satan is a liar and a deceiver and the only way he can have power over you is if you believe his lies."[4]

The first human sin was caused by a lie. Adam and Eve believed the serpent when he told them, "Eat the forbidden fruit. It's safe and will make you like God" (Gen. 3:4-5, paraphrased). Jesus further explained that some people "hear [the word of God], and then the devil comes and takes away the word from their hearts, so that they may not believe and be saved" (Luke 8:12). As soon as people are robbed of the word of God, they can no longer believe because they no longer know what is right to believe.

Satan's chief strategy is that he "blinds the minds of unbelievers" (2 Cor. 4:4; see also Eph. 2:2). Therefore, the divine weapons against him must demolish his arguments and pretensions:

> *The weapons we fight with are not the weapons of the world. On the contrary, they have divine power to demolish strongholds. We demolish arguments and every pretension that sets itself up against the knowledge of God, and we take captive every thought to make it obedient to Christ* (2 Corinthians 10:4-5).

When every thought is taken captive to the truth of Christ and is obedient to Him, then the victory is at hand because it is only the correct understanding of the truth that makes us see our need for Jesus.

However, the word of God as "the sword of the Spirit" accomplishes much more than the clarification of divine truth. As a weapon of the Spirit, the word of God comes with creative power and powerful confirmations of its divine origin. We prevail over satan's lies with the truth of God's word and also the power that comes with this word through the Holy Spirit. Thus, at one and the same time, we are engaged in a truth and power encounter with the forces of darkness.

In my seminary training, I learned that spiritual warfare was a truth encounter. The idea was that whatever was true was from God and was meant to prevail. However, spiritual warfare is more than a truth encounter because anyone with the truth alone, apart from the Spirit, cannot defeat satan's demons. Some fringe believers tried in the Bible, but were challenged by the demon and received "such a beating that they ran out of the house naked and bleeding" (Acts 19:16).

The word of God must be combined with the Spirit because only as the sword of the Spirit is it a most powerful weapon. This truth can be further demonstrated by listing numerous Bible references under three clarifying statements:

1. The word has no power without the Spirit.

   ...repentance and forgiveness of sins will be preached in his name to all nations...but stay in the city until you have been clothed with power from on high (Luke 24:45-49 NIV 1984).

   our gospel came to you not simply with words, but also with power, with the Holy Spirit and with deep conviction. ...you welcomed the message with the joy given by the Holy Spirit (1 Thessalonians 1:5-6 NIV 1984).

   See also Acts 1:4-8; Second Timothy 3:5; Zechariah 4:4.

2. The Spirit does nothing without the word.

   ...by God's word the heavens came into being and the earth was formed... (2 Peter 3:5).

   ...sustaining all things by his powerful word... (Hebrews 1:3)

   ...The words I have spoken to you—they are full of the Spirit and life (John 6:63).

   While Peter was still speaking these words, the Holy Spirit came on all who heard the message (Acts 10:44).

   you have been born...through the living and enduring word of God... (1 Peter 1:23-25).

   I will give you the keys of the kingdom of heaven; whatever you bind on earth will be bound in heaven, and whatever you loose on earth will be loosed in heaven (Matthew 16:19).

   ...just say the word and my servant will be healed (Matthew 8:8).

   ...he drove out the spirits with a word and healed all the sick (Matthew 8:16).

   See also Genesis 1:1-25; Psalm 107:20; Isaiah 55:10-11; Mark 7:33-35; Luke 8:4-15; John 20:22-23; Acts 6:7; 12:24; 19:20; Ephesians 5:26; 6:17; Philippians 2:15-16; Colossians 1:6; First Thessalonians 1:5-6,13; First Timothy

4:5; Second Timothy 4:1-2; Titus 1:3; Hebrews 4:12; James 1:18; Revelation 19:11-16.

3. The Spirit confirms the word with power.

> *...even though you do not believe me, believe the miracles, that you may know and understand that the Father is in me, and I in the Father* (John 10:38 NIV 1984).

> *...listen to this: Jesus...was a man accredited by God to you by miracles, wonders and signs, which God did among you through him, as you yourselves know* (Acts 2:22).

> *...the Lord who confirmed the message of his grace by enabling them to do miraculous signs and wonders* (Acts 14:3 NIV 1984).

> *Then the disciples went out and preached everywhere, and the Lord worked with them and confirmed his word by the signs that accompanied it* (Mark 16:20).

See also John 14:11-12; Acts 4:29-30; 8:6; Romans 15:18-19; First Corinthians 2:1-5; 4:20; Galatians 3:5; Hebrews 2:3-4.

There is nothing more useful than the word in resisting the fight-back attempts of the evil one. When the Spirit is upon the word, there is power in the declaration of truth so that the world is created out of nothing and even sins are forgiven. Signs and wonders follow and confirm the word. Apart from the Spirit, the word has no power; but as an instrument of the Spirit, it is a sword—a powerful weapon.

The Battle over Experience

The sword of the Spirit is a rather practical weapon and can be applied to one of the most common misconceptions of what it means to be filled and refilled with the Spirit and His power. Contrary to initial experiences and therefore common misconceptions, we do not always feel the power of the Spirit. We do not always sense heightened emotions when empowerment comes.

When Jesus and the disciples were first baptized with the Spirit, this was a powerful experience for them; and, likewise, Christians today seem to know when the first infilling of the Spirit happens to them.

Thus, Martyn Lloyd-Jones writes with confidence about experiencing the Spirit:

> It is that the baptism with the Holy Spirit [the initial filling with the Holy Spirit] is always something clear and unmistakable, something which can be recognized by the person to whom it happens and by others who look on at this person…The very essence of this is that it is conscious, that it is experimental, obvious, plain, and clear; not only to the recipient but also to those who are familiar with him…I am not concerned to emphasize anything spectacular, although we have got to say this: in the New Testament it was highly spectacular…to them…it was the most spectacular thing that had ever happened to them. So that any impression that is given that this is something quiet, and restrained and almost unobserved seems to me to be coming very near to what the apostle calls, "quenching the Spirit"…[5]

The evidence in the Bible supports Martyn Lloyd-Jones and his endorsement of even spectacular experiences. For some, the Holy Spirit came with a sound like the blowing of a violent wind, tongues of fire, and speaking in unknown tongues (see Acts 2:1-4). Others experienced an outburst of sudden praise, prophetic words, and speaking in tongues (see Acts 10:44-46; 19:6; 1 Thess. 1:5-6). In one instance, the Spirit came upon an entire congregation with such observable force that the preacher stopped his sermon (see Acts 10:44-46), and in another case, the apostle Paul even appealed to the experiences of his converts as evidence for his sound teaching. He wrote:

> *I would like to learn just one thing from you: Did you receive the Spirit by the works of the law, or by believing what you heard? So again I ask, does God give you his Spirit and work miracles among you by the works of the law, or by your believing what you heard?* (Galatians 3:2,5)

Paul's converts were to judge from the experiences of the Spirit whether his teaching was sound or not. Today, not many would try to win a theological argument in this way, but it represents a rather positive endorsement of Christian experience and validates the expectation that the Spirit keeps touching our senses and emotions. God keeps pouring out his love into our hearts through the Holy Spirit (see Rom.

5:5; see also Gal. 5:22-23), and He keeps assuring us of sonship with the sensation of hearing from Him since "the Spirit himself testifies with our spirit that we are God's children" (Rom. 8:16).

Yet, there is also another side to the Christian walk. Without minimizing or downgrading any previous statements, it is a mistake to base the entire Christian life on an experience. Watchman Nee warns repeatedly:

> ...The emotional part of the soul also can be aroused easily by the adversary. Since many believers crave joyful feelings and the sensations of having the Holy Spirit, of the loveliness of the Lord Jesus, and of the presence of God, evil spirits will supply their senses with many strange experiences. This is that their natural abilities might be stimulated and that the still small voice of the Holy Spirit, traceable only by a person's delicate intuitive faculty in his spirit, might be suppressed....[6]

These are words of wisdom. Not every spiritual experience is from God; on occasion, "Satan himself masquerades as an angel of light" (2 Cor. 11:14). Feelings, emotions, and sensations must always be tested and measured against the standard of the Scriptures (see Matt. 7:15-20; Acts 17:11; 1 Cor. 4:6; Gal. 1:8-9).

Furthermore, there are barren times when God Himself withdraws from Christians the comfort of experiencing Him. Jesus Himself had the greatest time when He was baptized with the Holy Spirit (see Luke 3:21-22). Jesus shared our humanity and must have enjoyed the tangible evidence of God's love. This divine encounter was amazing. He saw the Spirit and heard the audible voice of God the Father. But the emotional high was not to continue—it gave way to deprivations when he was led by the Spirit into the wilderness for forty days (see Luke 4:1-2).

Jesus remained full of the Holy Spirit but entered a season when exhilarating emotions were exchanged for hunger and temptations. Jesus became vulnerable, and the devil tried to exploit His stressed state of mind. He said, "Jesus, as Son of God, you shouldn't be feeling so miserable and hungry. This is not right and doesn't make sense. Turn these stones into bread" (Luke 4:3, paraphrased). A little later, the devil reasoned with Jesus again, "Your lonely wretchedness is not fitting for a Son of God. Worship me and I will make you enjoy power" (Luke 4:6-7; paraphrased). One more time, the devil said, "Jesus, why should you feel so low? If you are the Son of God, then more joyful experiences should be yours. Throw yourself down from a public building and soak up the adulation" (Luke 4:9-11, paraphrased).

The devil's strategy would have worked if Jesus had based His entire faith on emotions. Yet for all the positive assurances, we do not always feel and sense the Spirit even when He is present with us in power. Thus Jesus defeated the devil by taking the sword of the Spirit, which is the word of God, and quoted the Bible against the lies of satan. He marshalled the truth against any tempting lies—despite His feelings of hunger and hardship. For instance, He made powerful use of Deuteronomy 8:3 and said, "It is written: 'Man shall not live on bread alone, but on every word that comes from the mouth of God'" (Matt. 4:4; see also Luke 4:4,8,12).

We are to do the same as Jesus. We are to live on every word that comes from the mouth of God and not on our feelings. Previously, Jesus had heard the audible voice of God at His baptism with the Spirit, and He could look forward to further experiences of the same audible voice in His future ministry (see Luke 9:35; John 12:28), but in the wilderness, He was reduced to quoting what He had learned from the Scriptures. Sometimes the word of God can come to us with much inspiration and quickening emotions; but at other times, we must fall back on what we have learned in the past and trust the Scriptures even in barren seasons.

There are benefits in suffering the withdrawal of positive experiences. It builds character and redirects our affections toward God rather than His benefits. Madame Guyon was a woman who delighted in her experiences of God in prayer. However, God withdrew the wonderful taste of divine experiences and made her suffer for seven long years, after which He surprised her with an even deeper experience of Himself rather than His gifts. She writes in her autobiography:

> I fell into a state of total privation that lasted nearly seven years ... This state of emptiness, darkness, and impotency, went far beyond any trials I had ever yet met.[7]

I thought of nothing but ending my days thus. There remained in me not the least hope of ever emerging. ...I thought I had lost grace forever, and the salvation which it merits for us.[8]

[Then] on that happy Magdalene's Day my soul was perfectly delivered from all its pains...I was inexpressibly overjoyed to find Him, whom I thought I had lost forever, returned to me again with unspeakable magnificence and purity...All I had enjoyed before was only a peace, a gift of God, but now I received and possessed the God of peace.[9]

In losing all the gifts, with all their supports, I found the Giver...Oh, poor creatures, who pass all your time in feeding upon the gifts of God, and think therein to be the most favoured and happy, how I pity you if you stop here, short of the true rest, and cease to go forward to God Himself, through the loss of those cherished gifts which you now delight.[10]

Madame Guyon's privations are not unusual in the maturing life of Christians. Not everyone may suffer from dry spells that last for seven years, but there are wilderness periods for every believer.

Another testimony is from Graham Cooke who received the following word in the late 1970s.[11] God said to him, "Take a deep breath. For the next two years, you will not feel my presence. Learn this discipline. For the next two years, I will not let you sense any emotional or physical connection with me." In Graham's words, it took him six months to stop whining. He thought that if he whined long enough, God would change His mind but He did not. He had to learn and trust that God was present because He said so. When he laid hands on people, they would often fall to the floor, but he would not feel a thing. In the midst of great worship services, nothing stirred within him.

One day on tour, Graham took out a blank postcard from his briefcase, addressed it to God, and wrote in the message section, "Dear God, wish you were here. Love, Graham." He stuck the card in his Bible. A few days later, he accidentally knocked his Bible to the floor and the card floated to the ground. He looked at it. The message side was up and it read, "Dear Graham, what makes you think I'm not? Love,

God." He had written, "Dear God, wish you were here. Love, Graham." Now God messaged back, "Dear Graham, what makes you think I'm not? Love, God."

Graham looked at the card for about five minutes and then, according to his testimony, he saw the words change back to his own handwriting. He did not feel a thing. One day, he went to bed at 11 PM, suddenly woke up and the presence of God filled the room like a blanket. He looked at the clock and it was 12 PM—two years to the day—and God said, "Get up, son. We've got things to talk about."

God means to make the Christian life a rich experience of Him; but all the same, we cannot base our entire Christian walk on sensations of His goodness. When God tests our love for Him and weans us from the comfort of happy emotions, we rely on the sword of the Spirit to affirm the truth of His faithfulness and win the battle![12]

Endnotes

1. Hans-Werner Bartsch, ed., Reginald H. Fuller, trans., *Kerygma and Myth—A Theological Debate* (London, 1972), 5.

2. Friedemann Hebart, trans., *Luther's Large Catechism* (Adelaide, Australia: Lutheran Publishing House, 1983), 159-160.

3. Smith Wigglesworth, *Greater Works: Experiencing God's Power* (New Kensington, PA: Whitaker House, 1999), 78.

4. Neil Anderson, *The Steps to Freedom in Christ* (Ventura, CA: Gospel Light, 2001), 1.

5. D. Martyn Lloyd-Jones, *Joy Unspeakable: The Baptism and Gifts of the Holy Spirit* (Eastbourne, UK: Kingsway Publications, 1984), 52-54.

6. Watchman Nee, *The Spiritual Man* (New York: Christian Fellowship Publishers, 1977), Volume I, 177.

7. Jeanne Guyon, *Jeanne Guyon—An Autobiography* (New Kensington, PA: Whitaker House, 1997), 97.

8. Ibid., 116.

9. Ibid., 118.

10. Ibid., 120.

11. Graham Cooke, "Manifestation and Hiddenness," audio sermon.

12. Consider also Watchman Nee: "We know that the Lord at the commencement of our spiritual walk normally comforts us during those times we suffer on His behalf. He causes the unbeliever to sense His presence, see His smiling face, feel His love and experience His care in order to prevent him from fainting. When the believer apprehends the mind of the Lord and follows it He usually gives him great pleasure. Although he has paid some price for following the Lord yet the joy he obtains far surpasses what he has lost and hence he delights to obey His will. But the Lord perceives a danger here: upon having experienced comfort in suffering and happiness in heeding His mind, the child of God naturally looks for such comfort and joy the next time he suffers or obeys the Lord's will or else expects to be helped immediately by His comfort and joy. Hence he suffers or does the Lord's will not purely for His sake but for the sake of being rewarded with consolation and happiness as well. Without these crutches he is powerless to continue. The will of the Lord becomes inferior to the joy which He bestows at the moment of obedience.

God realizes His child is most eager to suffer if he is comforted, and is delighted to follow His will if he is accorded joy. But God now wishes to learn what motivates him: whether he suffers exclusively for the Lord's sake or for the sake of being consoled: whether he heeds God's mind because it should be heeded or because he derives some joy by so heeding. For this reason, after a Christian has made some progress spiritually God commences to withdraw the consolation and delight which He gave him in the hour of suffering and obedience. Now the Christian must suffer without any ministration of comfort from God: he suffers externally while feeling bitter inwardly. He is to do the will of God without the least thing to stimulate his interest; indeed everything is dry and uninteresting. By this process God will learn precisely why the believer suffers on His behalf and obeys His will. God is asking him: are you disposed to endure without being compensated by my comfort? Are you ready to endure just for Me? Are you amenable to perform labour which does not interest you a bit? Can you do it just because it is My purpose? Will you be able to undertake for Me when you feel depressed, insipid and parched? Can you do it simply because it is My work? Are you able to accept joyfully physical suffering without any compensation of refreshment? Can you accept it because it is given by Me?

This is a practical cross by which the Lord reveals to us whether we are living for Him by faith or living for ourselves by feeling..." Watchman Nee, *The Spiritual Man* Virginia, 1968, Volume II, 243-244.

Chapter 7

Speaking in Tongues Is a Gift

In 2005, forty Lutheran pastors from the state of Queensland met for a few days of professional development. At one stage, we conducted an anonymous survey into our prayer habits, and somehow the survey included the question, "Do you speak in tongues?" Thirty pastors filled out the survey and, to everyone's surprise, ten out of the thirty, one-fourth of all Lutheran pastors present, replied that they did. That many spoke in tongues; yet no one knew who they were. Why? Because, for whatever reason, we Lutherans in Australia remain uneasy about this spiritual gift; therefore, we remain uneasy about admitting to this spiritual gift as if speaking in tongues undermined sound doctrines.

A year later, another colleague came up to me at our denomination's General Synod meeting and he confided in me, "I also speak in tongues, but I keep it quiet." Why would anyone want to keep quiet about a gift from God? There is a compelling reason. People like to protect their reputation. No one likes to be judged by the mainline churches and be counted among the "weird people." Furthermore, there are those who are more relaxed about the gift but are sharing my former attitude. I simply did not want to pray words that I did not understand. What possible purpose can it serve?

A Biblical Survey

A brief survey of the Bible reveals that the main sources of information about the gift of speaking in tongues come from the book of Acts and the first letter to the Corinthians. In the book of Acts,

SURPRISED *by the* HOLY SPIRIT

the gift is closely associated with the infilling of the Holy Spirit. Thus, on the day of Pentecost, the first disciples received what was promised to them by Jesus: "All of them were filled with the Holy Spirit and began to speak in other tongues [other languages] as the Spirit enabled them" (Acts 2:4).

Likewise, in Acts 10, the gift of speaking in tongues came with the Spirit baptism and functioned as a sign of that immersion in the Spirit:

> *While Peter was still speaking these words, the Holy Spirit came on all who heard the message. The circumcised believers who had come with Peter were astonished that the gift of the Holy Spirit had been poured out even on Gentiles. For they heard them speaking in tongues and praising God* (Acts 10:44-46).

In similar fashion, Acts 19:6 connects the first infilling of the Spirit with the release of the gift of tongues and prophecy, "When Paul placed his hands on them, the Holy Spirit came on them, and they spoke in tongues and prophesied."

In First Corinthians, there are further references to speaking in tongues, and they affirm the gift:

> *And in the church God has appointed...those speaking in different kinds of tongues* (1 Corinthians 12:28 NIV 1984).

> *...eagerly desire gifts of the Spirit...For anyone who speaks in a tongue...they utter mysteries by the Spirit. ...Anyone who speaks in a tongue edifies themselves...I would like every one of you to speak in tongues...* (1 Corinthians 14:1-5).

> *For this reason the one who speaks in a tongue should pray that they may interpret what they say. For if I pray in a tongue, my spirit prays, but my mind is unfruitful. So what shall I do? I will pray with my spirit, but I will also pray with my understanding; I will sing with my spirit, but I will also sing with my understanding* (1 Corinthians 14:13-15).

> *I thank God that I speak in tongues more than all of you* (1 Corinthians 14:18).

> *...do not forbid speaking in tongues* (1 Corinthians 14:39).[1]

From this brief survey, we can conclude that, against all possible protestations, Christians must come to grips with the strange phenomenon of speaking in tongues. In the book of Acts, more than once, all who were filled with the Spirit spoke in tongues—every one! Then, the book of First Corinthians commands us not to forbid speaking in tongues but eagerly desire spiritual gifts. Apostle Paul said without any hesitation, "I would like every one of you to speak in tongues," and he thanked God that he himself was speaking more in tongues than anyone else at Corinth. Thus, we may hear a definition of what may happen even in our own lives: "Speaking in tongues is a supernatural manifestation of the Holy Spirit, whereby the believer speaks forth in a language he has never learned and that he does not understand."[2]

Two Divisive Questions

Before unpacking some of the uses and purposes of speaking in tongues, we will tackle two of the most divisive questions associated with this spiritual gift. Here is the first one: Must everyone speak in tongues? The answer is no. Speaking in tongues is not necessary for one's salvation.[3] The Bible affirms that "whoever believes and is baptized will be saved" (Mark 16:16). As a Christian, anyone can be certain that it is "by grace you have been saved through faith" (Eph. 2:8). Thus, the key to salvation is faith in Jesus Christ—not speaking in tongues.

Furthermore, when the apostle Paul wrote to the Corinthians, there seemed to be believers who had not received the gift of speaking in tongues or were at least not functioning in the gift for the wider community. He wrote:

> And God has placed in the church first of all apostles, second prophets, third teachers, then miracles, then gifts of healing, of helping, of guidance, and of different kinds of tongues. Are all apostles? Are all prophets? Are all teachers? Do all work miracles? Do all have gifts of healing? Do all speak in tongues? Do all interpret? (1 Corinthians 12:28-30).

There was only ever one answer to all of these questions. It was no. Apostle Paul and the congregation in Corinth were in agreement: "No, not all are apostles! No, not all are prophets! No, not all speak in tongues!" The gift of speaking in tongues, in this context of other service gifts, was not given to everyone; but Paul encouraged all church members to want more than they had at present and "eagerly desire spiritual gifts" (1 Cor. 14:1).

Thus, we can say with confidence that not everyone must speak in tongues because it is not a matter of salvation—but how many could? If all Christians desired the spiritual gift of speaking in tongues, how many of us would end up receiving the gift? Judging by my own limited experience and the experience of many churches over the past one hundred years, the gift of speaking in tongues is not a rare gift. Nicky Gumbel[4] calls it a "beginner's gift," which is frequently given to brand-new believers as it accompanies and confirms the infilling of the Holy Spirit.[5] There is really no maturity level required; and in Acts, on different occasions, all believers—without exception—seemed to have received that gift all at once.

According to National Church Life Survey data from 1996 (Australia), about 10 percent of attendees in the Catholic, Anglican, Uniting, and other larger non-Pentecostal denominations speak in tongues, which compares with a 17 percent approval level of that gift among Lutherans. Overall, 14 percent of church attendees speak in tongues, which compares with a 27 percent approval level across the denominations.[6]

Now this data could be interpreted in the sense that whoever approves of the gift has a good chance of actually speaking in tongues himself. There is not such a wide percentage margin between gift approval and the actual speaking in tongues (7 and 13 percentage points respectively), which once again points to the spiritual "success rate" of the First Corinthians 14:1 instruction, "eagerly desire spiritual gifts."[7] If people approve of the gift and also desire it with eagerness and persistence, then they seem to have a good chance of actually speaking in tongues themselves.

Nicky Gumbel writes:

> Not every Christian speaks in tongues. Yet Paul says: "I would like every one of you to speak in tongues," suggesting that it is not only for a special class of Christians. It is open to all Christians. There is no reason why anyone who wants this gift should not receive it.[8]

In summary, not everyone must speak in tongues because it is not necessary for one's salvation but, at the same time, it is not a rare gift. However, what complicates matters is the common observation that the baptism with the Spirit and the release of the gift of tongues often coincide and, at times, even seem to hinge on each other. Thus, not everyone must speak in tongues for salvation, but the baptism with the Spirit often calls for the believer's cooperation in receiving this gift.

This, then, is the second divisive question associated with the gift: Must a Christian speak in tongues at his or her baptism with the Spirit?

I may immediately clarify that there is no hard and fast rule. Randy Clark, whom God used to start the movement of the Toronto Blessing, is convinced that he received the gift of tongues before his Spirit baptism, and he writes in more general terms: "I don't believe one must speak in tongues to be baptized in the Spirit."[9]

When an American theologian listened to the stories of a black pastor in Mozambique and heard how the Lord had used him to raise seven people from the dead, he was amazed. Then he had the following light hearted encounter: "I asked if he and the gathered prayed more in Makua, their heart-language, or in tongues. He grinned sheepishly: 'I cannot lie. I have never prayed in tongues.' Heidi [Baker] and I roared with laughter—that sure puts a dinger in the *initial evidence* theology of the baptism of the Spirit."[10]

God can fill people with the Spirit to the brim so that they can raise the dead in Jesus' name and this can happen without the gift of speaking in tongues. I am sure that my own daughter Francisca was immersed in the Spirit at the age of twelve when she fell down under the power of the Spirit and remained unconscious for a long time. There was rapid eye movement and a deep encounter with God, but no gift of tongues. Thus, in light of all of these testimonies and no explicit requirement in the Bible, it would be unwise to insist that the baptism with the Spirit always coincides with the release of the gift of tongues.

On the other hand, however, there are the Scripture passages that suggest a common connection between the baptism with the Spirit and the spiritual gift of speaking in tongues. At least in the experience of the early church, many who received the immersion in the Spirit

SURPRISED *by the* HOLY SPIRIT

also began to speak in tongues (see Acts 2:1-4; 10:44-46; 19:1-6). David Pawson sums up the biblical evidence in this way:

> Tongues...Fluent speech in a language never before either learned or spoken is obviously a supernatural endowment. This is the most common [outward] evidence mentioned [in the Bible for the infilling with the Spirit] and should not be treated with suspicion or contempt. It can encourage people to believe that the Spirit enables them to go beyond their natural ability, leading them into other 'spiritual gifts' (Greek *charismata*, from which 'charismatic' is derived).
>
> But to insist that it must always be such 'tongues' is to be narrower than the scripture. While it may be more frequent than any other form of inspired speech, that does not warrant the demand that it *must* be this gift, as *the* 'initial evidence.' Other 'overflows' are mentioned—for example, 'praise' and 'prophecy,' both of which are in a known and familiar language.[11]

This is a balanced statement, but nevertheless points out that the release of the gift of tongues was common at the believers' baptism with the Spirit. Thus it is not unreasonable to expect the same today. There are entire Christian denominations that observe almost everyone in their midst is receiving this gift.

In my own limited experience, I have encountered many Lutherans who told me, "I am ready for anything from God—except the gift of tongues. I want to be immersed in the Spirit, but not speak in unknown languages." In these Lutherans, there were problems in overcoming past prejudice and the fear of the unknown. There was pride that did not want to yield to the "babbling" of the Spirit.

In almost every instance, God did not accept the human condition that was placed on the outpouring of the Spirit. He usually required that there was a movement from fear to faith and from pride to humility. Then, as people let go of control, absolutely surrendered, and submitted even their tongues to God, the Spirit baptism would occur easily, without striving. The Spirit would bubble forth freely in them when He was allowed to express Himself through their tongues.

At one of our Prayer Watch meetings, I sensed that I should ask a visitor whether he spoke in tongues. He said that he had not yet received this gift. I then asked him whether we could pray for him. He consented to prayer, and then we prayed for him with our hands on his head and shoulders. After a while, we stepped back and I asked him what occurred for him. He said that he felt a tingling all over his body and it rose up to his head. Then, something seemed to lift up his tongue but instead of speaking out words, he stopped the experience because he became afraid. He thanked us for the prayers, but did not want to try again.

Many a time, like in this testimony, believers do have the power to stop the experience of receiving more from the Spirit or being baptized with Him because they can resist the Spirit's movements by pulling themselves up and yielding to their own fear or pride rather than the Spirit.

Thus, in conclusion to these thoughts, I would encourage all Christians to take note of the common connection between the baptism with the Spirit and the gift of speaking in tongues and prepare themselves for an experience that may require them to be both foolish and humble:

> *For the foolishness of God is wiser than human wisdom, and the weakness of God is stronger than human strength* (1 Corinthians 1:25).[12]

Purposeful Tongues

What is the use of speaking in tongues? There is more than one use but the most common purpose seems to be the provision of a language or languages for prayer. As we pray in tongues, we express all possible prayer forms such as praise, adoration, thanksgiving, confession, intercession, and petition (see 1 Cor. 14:15-17).

The Bible further explains that "if I pray in a tongue, my spirit prays, but my mind is unfruitful" (1 Cor. 14:14). The gift of praying in tongues leaves the mind unfruitful, which means that the mind does not understand the words and this in itself can be good.

Lutheran pastor Larry Christenson writes:

> It would seem that prayer in which the mind is unfruitful would have little value. What blessing can it be to pray when

you have no idea what you are praying about? Actually, this is one of its greatest blessings—the fact that it is not subject to the limitations of your human intellect. The human mind, wonderful as it is from the hand of the Creator, has limited knowledge, limited linguistic ability, limited understanding, and furthermore is inhibited with all manner of prejudice, little and large. Speaking in tongues is a God-appointed manner of praying that can bypass the limitations of the intellect. One may picture the difference something like this: A prayer with the mind comes upward from the heart and must then pass through a maze of linguistic, theological, rational, emotional and personal checkpoints before it is released upward. By the time "it gets out," it may be little more than a slender trickle. An utterance in tongues comes upward from the depths, but instead of being channelled through the mind, it bypasses the mind and flows directly to God in a stream of Spirit-prompted prayer, praise and thanksgiving.[13]

The gift of speaking in tongues bypasses the mind and thus bypasses the limitations of our intellectual filters. Most of all, it gives God free access to overwhelm us with His grace—rather than self-condemnation—so that "Anyone who speaks in a tongue edifies themselves" (1 Cor. 14:4; see also Jude 1:20). For instance, my friend (Pastor Ian Shelton) often tells me that if he is feeling tired before an evening meeting, he lies on his bed, prays in tongues for about ten minutes, and then gets up refreshed. He has learned to "edify himself" in God.

Now the benefits of bypassing our minds goes even further. The Bible declares that "anyone who speaks in a tongue does not speak to people but to God. Indeed, no one understands them; they utter mysteries by the Spirit" (1 Cor. 14:2). People, who pray in tongues, do not understand the words and, therefore, they certainly utter "mysteries" to their human minds. The whole exercise must seem mysterious to them and others.

However, this is not the meaning of the Bible verse. The "mysteries" that are uttered by the Spirit are rather the deep things of God. In the Bible, the word "mysteries" can function as a more technical term for the truth, knowledge, and will of God so that the apostle Paul called church leaders like himself "servants of Christ and as those entrusted with the mysteries God has revealed" (1 Cor. 4:1).[14] Thus when we pray in tongues, our speaking somehow connects us with the deep wisdom of God and makes us penetrate the mysteries of His truth, knowledge, and will. This has an effect. As the Holy Spirit is revealing mysteries to our spirit, revelation can then flow from our spirit to the mind (see also 1 Cor. 2:6-16).

One pastor believes that the apostle Paul "prayed in the spirit until the 'mysteries' of God began to come alive in his spirit, then as revelation came he wrote them down."[15] According to the same pastor, the speaking of tongues can be a key to opening the realm of the Spirit where the Holy Spirit is leading and guiding us into all truth.[16] This may also explain the observation that the gift of tongues is usually followed by other emerging spiritual gifts—especially the prophetic gifts.

In this respect, I am thankful for the gift of tongues when I am praying over people. At times, I do not know how to proceed in prayer, so I simply switch from English into the gift of tongues. After a while, I find that I am again receiving revelatory impressions for the person in front of me and can continue in English. For me, it is of immense help to let the Spirit direct the prayer ministry.

Another scholar points out that speaking in tongues "…appears to answer the need of the [human] spirit to express the inexpressible, to carry the dialogue with God beyond the narrow limits of clearly intelligible language."[17] The Bible says in similar fashion that "…the Spirit helps us in our weakness. We do not know what we ought to pray for, but the Spirit himself intercedes for us through wordless groans" (Rom. 8:26).

The following is a testimony from my friend and Lutheran colleague Dirk Willner. On Good Friday 2004, at the age of forty, he died while in the hospital and remained dead for about two minutes. He suffered from "sick-sinus-syndrome" which is a shut-down of the electrical system in the body. Thus, from one moment to the next, he died; but owing to a number of fortunate "coincidences," he was already under observation in the hospital. The medical staff saved him, and he returned with a story to tell about heaven. He was saturated with the glory of God (a golden substance that looked like honey), was bathed in joy, stepped into the welcoming hall in heaven (glistening and glittering with gold and jewels), saw a great multitude of people dressed in white, met Jesus whose appearance was an intense dazzling light, and talked with Him.

Because this was an amazing and unusual experience, it took Dirk awhile to muster the courage and share his story with other Christians. However, this is not all that happened. In his time of recovery, God also gave him revelation about the gift of tongues. I have permission to quote from his personal account:

> I would walk around the house aimlessly, privately reflecting on what had happened to me. It was hard at first even to take Penne [my wife] into my confidence and tell her about what I saw in heaven. On this particular day, my in-laws were visiting to see how I was recovering. During the afternoon they felt that they could leave me for a while and drive down to the beach for a coffee at one of the many cafes. I was sitting upright in my bed, dressed; it was midafternoon.
>
> Once the whole family left, I spent some time in prayer, just chatting to Him about this heavenly encounter. The experience was so puzzling to me. I was confused and questioned its purpose as to why this kind of incident took place. I remember saying something like, "Well God, I know You can switch me off and on, but what's the point of demonstrating that to me? What did You have in mind in sharing this? I already know that You have all of life and death in Your hands. I believe heaven exists!"
>
> Suddenly, and I have to reiterate that I was wide awake, a group of five angels appeared around my bed. Each angel was standing tall and independent, but united in purpose. They looked larger than humans and broader across the shoulders. Their stature was strong and instantly gave the appearance of a force to be reckoned with.
>
> The angels' appearance was impressive. They seemed to be full of sparkle; every inch of their bodies were radiating a vibrant sparkling energy. I remember that they gave the impression of being very task-orientated; there seemed to be

very little interest in chitchat. Apparently no introductions were necessary.

The angel on my right side seemed to have had a higher rank, and I say that simply because he took the lead with this question: "What instructions have you got for us?" I could hear him as clearly as if I was having a conversation with a friend right there in the room with me. I responded with surprise: "Instructions? I don't give you instructions. If you want instructions go to God, He will give you instructions."

He leaned forward and said: "Give me your hand!" I remember seeing his hand as he stretched it out toward me. I could see the same anatomy as that of a human being; my eyes examined the features—five fingers, just like us, a hand, just like us, an arm, just like us. It was fascinating. I thought to myself, *Well, I'll see where this will go,* and put my right hand into his. It was a firm handshake.

Immediately I was speaking a heavenly language. It just started to come out of me as if I had always known it. The words were articulate. There was a distinct sentence structure. But I had no way of knowing what was being said. I remember God speaking into my mind saying, "Don't worry, you know that I give this gift through My Spirit as I will. I am giving instructions to the angels through you."

As I had finished giving instructions to the first angel, then the second one put out his hand. Again I put my own hand into his and began speaking yet another completely different language—and the same for each of the other angels.

When I had finished giving them instructions as the Holy Spirit enabled me, they vanished. They just turned around and could not be seen anymore. But right there sitting at the end of my bed was a sixth angel, much less war-like and imposing in his appearance; very personable and friendly. I said to him, "And what can I do for you?" He simply replied, "Nothing, I'm here for you." Then he too vanished, and I continued on in prayer. Now really perplexed and confused as to what I had just seen and participated in. *This is going to be really hard to explain,* was a constant thought, *what would people think about this?* More importantly, *What should I make of all this?*[18]

As Dirk and the five angels exchanged firm handshakes, Dirk began to speak in all of the five languages of the different angels. They were different from each other and they also served different purposes. He figured out that one was for healing, one was for rebuking satan, one was for undoing the works of satan, one was for praising God, and one was simply for having a chat with God. Dirk is still speaking these five languages today and he can even pray these languages in his mind—without speaking them aloud. This even amazed his Pentecostal friends.

May everyone be encouraged to seek the gift of speaking in tongues and then use it in persistent and persevering prayer. What can be better than healing, rebuking, and undoing the works of satan, praising God, and having a chat with Him? The experience of Dirk Willner also throws light on another pastor's testimony. This pastor experienced a transformation in ministry through the use of speaking in tongues; he writes:

> By the clock I prayed 15 minutes a day in the language of the Spirit and still felt nothing as I asked the Spirit to help me intercede for those he wanted to reach. After about six weeks of this I began to lead people to Jesus without trying. Gangsters fell to their knees sobbing in the streets, women were healed, heroin addicts were miraculously set free. And I knew it all had nothing to do with me.[19]

Another altogether different use of speaking in tongues is for God to convey messages to others. According to the Bible, this is what happened on the day of Pentecost: "All of them were filled with the Holy Spirit and began to speak in other tongues as the Spirit enabled them" (Acts 2:4). A gathering of peasant Christians suddenly spoke or were heard speaking in foreign languages. This caused a reaction among the audience:

> *Utterly amazed* [those listening] *asked, "…how is it that each of us hears them in his own native language? …we hear them declaring the wonders of God in our own tongues!"* (Acts 2:7-11)

This is still happening today. For instance, Pastor Dave Roberson noticed that every time he made a statement, a man about three rows from the front would bend over and whisper to the man next to him. His righteous indignation began to be stirred up. He was getting irritated and thought, "If they're going to interrupt the service, the least they could do is sit in the back." Somewhere in the middle of his message, the two men stopped whispering to each other and this helped the preacher to concentrate. After the service the preacher was in the back room recovering when someone else came in asking, "Did you notice those two men who were whispering to each other during the service?" He replied, "Yes. They talked about a third of the way through the message and then stopped." "Well, one of them only speaks French. He brought his own translator so he could enjoy the service." The preacher started to feel badly about his irritation. Then the person added, "This Frenchman said that one third of the way through the service, you stopped preaching in English and started to preach in French." He protested, "But I didn't preach in French." "Well, he says you did." It turned out that the message this person heard in French was the same that was delivered in English. God repeated the miracle of making people hear His word in their own tongues.[20]

Far more examples could be added with lots of different variations. Another common experience is when people may speak in a tongue unknown to them but communicating to a native speaker of that language in the auditorium. Nicky Gumbel tells the story of an English girl praying in tongues over a friend. This made her friend smile because the words spoken in tongues turned out to be Russian, and the friend receiving prayer was Russian. Thus, she was hearing from God in a supernatural way—again and again: "My dear child. My dear child."[21]

Then, the Bible spends more time giving instructions of how a message spoken in tongues may be interpreted by the same person or another person: "…anyone who speaks in a tongue should pray that he may interpret what he says" (1 Cor. 14:13 NIV 1984). In worship services, the speaking in tongues with subsequent interpretations used to be a regular occurrence in an ordered way, "If anyone speaks in a tongue, two—or at the most three—should speak, one at a time, and someone must interpret" (1 Cor. 14:27).

A few years ago, I was holding another Holy Spirit seminar. As I was praying for a young woman at the end of the day, I was praying over her in tongues. Later she told me that she could understand what

I was saying. All during the day, she had been struggling with God. She was envious of other Christians who had been born to good parents who instructed them in the faith. She accused God of not looking after her. Then she repented and humbled herself before God. When I finally prayed over her in tongues, she heard God telling her that she was His princess. He was her Father and was looking after her. These words overwhelmed her, but I had no idea.

At this point, the whole matter of speaking in tongues may have become a little confusing. With so many uses for the one gift, how can we know what happens when? God will need to be our guide and maybe we can relax in Him because we do not have to be in control. However, I repeat that one of the key uses of speaking in tongues is simply the provision of a language or languages for prayer, and these language(s) for prayer seem to operate more in the privacy of our own homes rather than in public, "He who speaks in a tongue edifies himself" (1 Cor. 14:4 NIV 1984).

Receiving the Gift

How do we receive the gift of speaking in tongues? If you want the gift, how can you attain it? Once again, there does not seem to be a fixed method that God employs to bestow that gift upon us. Some receive it literally in their sleep waking up one day with a foreign tongue on their lips. Others seek and desire for years before they receive. I myself never wanted to speak in tongues, but one day opened my mouth in a prayer meeting and out came a fully formed language, which was unknown to me.

At the same time, my wife had been longing and waiting for this gift for two years. When she finally received this gift, she did not immediately speak in tongues fluently but was given just one word. It took days and weeks for more words to come and form a language. While I never consciously thought about any word that was flowing from my mouth, my wife knew beforehand the first word she was to speak out. God impressed it on her mind. Thus, the experiences of receiving the gift of tongues vary because our God is creative and cannot be contained or controlled by fixed methods.

Another colleague and friend received the gift of tongues at the age of four. His father was speaking in tongues in a worship service and he simply tried to copy the words. While he was trying to do so, he received the gift himself. An older farmer told me that everyone around him was beginning to speak in tongues, and this included his wife. He became annoyed that he seemed to be the only one missing out. Therefore, he sat down on a log one day and said to God in the middle of the paddock, "I will not get up and leave this place until you give me the gift of speaking in tongues." He was sitting on the log for a few hours but finally received what he was asking for.

Not that long ago, one of our younger church members also decided to pray earnestly for the gift of speaking in tongues. In the middle of the night, she became quite intense in her petitioning of God, but she was beginning to get into a striving attitude where she was tempted to rely on her own efforts of praying rather than trying to receive the gift by faith. When she finally gave up her striving, sat down on a lounge chair and became still before God, He released the gift to her. It was not hard but easy. The next morning, her husband and Lutheran parents were quite amazed that they now had a tongue-speaking Christian among them.

The experiences of receiving this spiritual gift vary, but there is no need to become confused. God is the giver of the gift, and we can trust His guidance, which is gentle most of the time. The advice is to remain sensitive to the promptings of the Holy Spirit. Thus, a Lutheran pastor writes:

> Many people expect to be seized upon, overwhelmed, and virtually compelled to speak in tongues. But this is not the way the Spirit treats us. He leads, He encourages, He prompts, He gives—but He does not force.
>
> The prompting may be a syllable, a word, or a phrase in the mind; to the understanding it is a meaningless sound, but when spoken out it leads into a new tongue. Or, it may be a certain "moving of the Spirit" upon the tongue or lips, which will form into syllables and words as one lends the voice. Or, it may be a spontaneous speaking forth, difficult to describe because it is so personal. People's experiences of just how it begins seem to vary greatly. Once begun, however, the phenomenon is fairly consistent: A spontaneous and usually

fluent language, in which the words are prompted not by the mind but by the Spirit.[22] Once a person has spoken in tongues, he may do so at will thereafter."[23]

Virtually everyone agrees that the gift of speaking in tongues has to be received by faith because this is the foundational principle of receiving anything from God:

> *And without faith it is impossible to please God, because anyone who comes to him must believe that he exists and that he rewards those who earnestly seek him* (Hebrews 11:6).

This means that we need to exercise and cultivate a certain faith expectation and then step out according to our faith expectation. In the case of speaking in tongues, this means that we cooperate with the Spirit and begin formulating words expecting them to be shaped by the Spirit according to our faith.

When I received this gift, I started out saying the word "Jesus" and then let the sound of the word linger until additional words formed and were flowing from my mouth. I encourage you not to be afraid and not to demand perfection immediately. It is okay when the first few words are simply words and sounds which come from one's own initiative. As we give Jesus our tongues, He can take over and transform any human babble into the spiritual gift of speaking in tongues. The truth is that no one can expect to receive the gift by keeping their mouths firmly shut.

Ultimately, it is simple. We trust that God delights in giving give good gifts to His children, and we know that speaking in tongues is one of these gifts (see Matt. 7:11). Sometimes God is bestowing this gift upon an entire body of believers (see Acts 2:4; 10:44-46; 19:6). Thus, we pray with faith and expectation. Another Christian who has already received the gift may pray with us and for us. Our thoughts focus on Jesus. Then we make a sound and trust that Jesus will give us the words and shape the words into a language.

Our faith can be an adventure. If anyone does not receive at once, he may check whether this is God's sovereign choice or maybe there is something in him blocking the release of the gift; for example, unbelief, fear, feelings of inadequacy, unforgiveness. However, the key is to keep trusting the love of God and not beat ourselves up over any delays. We are promised that the Spirit keeps working in us and that God's timing is always perfect.

Two Temptations

There are two almost universal temptations that are trouble Christians who have received the gift of speaking in tongues. The first temptation comes at once and consists of thinking that we are fabricating the "gibberish" ourselves. In my experience, every new tongue-speaking Christian suffers through a period of uncertainty, questioning the genuineness of the gift. Another pastor explains why:

> This is a natural thought, for the interaction between the believer and the Holy Spirit is so subtle that it is hard to draw a clear line between my speaking and His prompting. The temptation, when this thought comes, is to draw back and deny the gift, or to quit using it. Our ultimate confidence cannot be the experience itself, but God's Word…He has promised not to give me a stone when I ask for bread (Matthew 7:9)…As you continue to use the gift, you will pass through this test….[24]

With practice, the believer learns to appreciate that he is not making up the words and sounds. In many ways, this can be compared to other experiences where the demarcation line between God's activity and ours is thin. For instance, it took me a long time to recognize that the "flowing thoughts" on my prayer walks were not distractions but God's way of communicating His thoughts to me. I used to become frustrated when I was drifting from intercession to sermon ideas or general church business. However, the sermon ideas were often "out of this world," and I began to pay attention. In time, the spiritual gift of tongues does become established in the same way. We are not making up the words but they are flowing from a different source, which is God.

There is a second temptation that comes to bother most Christians who have received the gift of speaking in tongues. While there may be some initial excitement over the Spirit-given words, the initial enthusiasm often wanes because this gift does not come with the hoped-for "wow factor." The emotional state of praying in tongues is the same as praying in English or any other known language. Sometimes there is a sense of being charged with the presence of God but, at other times, we are still drawing near to Him in praise and repentance. It is usually a process to leave our worries and business behind and experience intimacy with God.

At first, many Christians are thrilled to receive the gift of speaking in tongues but then realize that this gift does not guarantee greater emotional highs. Thus they begin to battle some disappointment, which is made worse by possible boredom. Since the mind is not engaged in the gift of speaking in tongues, the mind of many is becoming bored with the exercise. It is a revelation to many Christians that the continued practice of praying in tongues requires discipline and perseverance. When I first received the gift, I was certainly bored with the use of the gift. It took me months to incorporate the praying in tongues into my regular prayer habits. I had to remind myself that God probably gave me the gift for a reason; therefore, I better steward what He has given me.

My encouragement for you is to keep using the gift because the promises and blessings of God do not depend on our feelings. Remember, the apostle Paul wrote, "I would like every one of you to speak in tongues…" (1 Cor. 14:5).

ENDNOTES

1. One needs to acknowledge that the phenomenon of speaking in tongues may also be caused by demonic forces, and thus the Bible warns us in First John 4:1, "…do not believe every spirit, but test the spirits to see whether they are from God…."

2. Larry Christenson, *Answering Your Questions About Speaking in Tongues* (Minneapolis, MN: Bethany House, 1968), 22.

3. For instance, such godly men as Martin Luther, Charles Spurgeon, John Wesley, John Knox, George Whitefield, Charles Finney, D.L. Moody, and others did not speak in tongues. See John Rice, *The Charismatic Movement* (Murfreesboro, TN: Sword of the Lord Publishers, 1976), 78-80.

4. One may also notice how the apostle Paul rated this spiritual gift last in two enumerations of spiritual gifts in First Corinthians 12:8-10,28.

5. Nicky Gumbel is an ordained Anglican priest, vicar, and author. He is most famous as the developer of the Alpha course, a basic introduction to Christianity supported by churches of many Christian traditions.

6. About half (52 percent) are neutral or do not have a view on the matter. And 21 percent oppose speaking in tongues.

7. One may also consider that not everyone who approves of speaking in tongues may actually seek that gift for himself.

8. Nicky Gumbel, *Questions of Life—A Practical Introduction to the Christian Faith* (Colorado Springs, CO: Cook Communication Ministries, 1993), 159.

9. Randy Clark, *Baptism in the Spirit* (Mechanicsburg, PA: Global Awakening 2006), 30.

10. Guy Chevreau, *Turnings—The Kingdom of God and the Western World* (Tonbridge, UK: Sovereign World, 2004), 55. At the end of the conversation, the pastor was prayed for and received the gift of tongues.

11. David Pawson, *Jesus Baptizes in One Holy Spirit* (London: Hodder & Stoughton, 1997), 122-123.

12. Father Robert DeGrandis contends: "The first gift to focus on after baptism in the Spirit would be the gift of tongues. This gift seems to be the 'cork in the bottle.' Once tongues is released, other gifts begin to flow." Father Robert DeGrandis with Mrs Linda Schubert, *Come, Follow Me* (USA, 1989), 50. This observation may have some merit because especially this gift seems to humble our intellectual pride and thus makes room for the operation of the Spirit according to His will rather than ours.

Ernest Gentile writes: "Speaking in tongues is quite a remarkable idea when you consider the physical process. God gives evidence of the inner presence of the Spirit by using the body member most dependent on volitional, human intelligence: the tongue! 'No man can tame the tongue. It is an unruly evil, full of deadly poison' (James 3:8). God controls the most rebellious member of the human body (and by implication, all the others). Bypassing the mind, the Spirit uses the tongue to glorify God in words unknown to the person's brain, and thus, not corrupted by any self-serving motivation. Speaking in tongues allows an individual to pray words undefiled, because it is the Spirit Himself who directs the utterance." Ernest Gentile, *The Glorious Disturbance—Understanding and Receiving the Baptism with the Spirit* (Grand Rapids, MI: Chosen Books, 2004), 111-112.

"The willingness to surrender our tongues to God may also indicate a more profound surrender than almost any other act. The tongue is the primary instrument of expression of the human personality, and until God has dominion over the tongue, His control over us is relatively slight." Don Basham, *A Handbook on Holy Spirit Baptism* (Pittsburgh, PA: Whitaker House 1969), 91.

13. Larry Christenson, *Answering Your Questions About Speaking in Tongues* (Minneapolis, MN: Bethany House, 1968), 73-74.

14. Compare First Corinthians 2:7-14 from the New King James Version: "But we speak the wisdom of God in a mystery…which none of the rulers of this age knew…But God has revealed *them* to us through his Spirit. For the Spirit searches all things, yes, the deep things of God. …no one knows the things of God except the Spirit of God. Now we have received, not the spirit of the world, but the Spirit who is from God, that we might know the things that have been freely given to us by God. … the things of the Spirit of God…are spiritually discerned." Also compare Ephesians 3:9; 6:9 and Colossians 1:26.

15. Col Stringer, *Praying in the Spirit—Tongues for Personal Edification* (Australia: Col Stringer Ministries, 1995), 20.

16. Ibid., 24.

17. Paul Tournier quoted in Larry Christenson's *Answering Your Questions About Speaking in Tongues* (Minneapolis, MN: Bethany House, 1968), 26.

18. Dirk Willner, A Personal Account of a Near Death Experience with a Heavenly Vision and Followed Up with Angelic Visitations (Gold Coast, 2009). See www.livinggracetoowoomba.org/2009/2009TestimonyDirkWillner.pdf. See also, www.life-beyondnow.com.

19. Jack Pullinger quoted in Nicky Gumbel, *Questions of Life—A Practical Introduction to the Christian Faith* (Colorado Springs, CO: Cook Communication Ministries, 1993), 158.

20. Dave Roberson, *The Walk of the Spirit—The Walk of Power* (Tulsa, OK: Dave Roberson Ministries), 103-104.

21. Nicky Gumbel, *Questions of Life*, 155.

22. Christenson, *Answering Your Questions About Speaking in Tongues*, 125-126. According to Christenson, speaking in tongues has the same emotional potential as speech or prayer in one's native tongue (24).

23. Ibid., 130.

24. Ibid., 131.

Appendix A

Practical Encouragement

Many books are written on the subject of the Holy Spirit, and their complexities may intimidate the new Christian. However, it is not hard to receive an infilling of the Spirit because Jesus is in charge of the experience and He does not require our perfect understanding before He releases the fullness of the Spirit on us. As we repent and trust Him, we are ready and can relax in His goodness. He is faithful and will baptize us in the Spirit as promised.

There are instances where people are filled with the Spirit in the privacy of their own personal devotions, but the common practice in the Bible was the release of the Spirit through the prayer(s) of other Spirit-filled Christians. This is still the easiest way to receive an infilling of the Holy Spirit.

In my own limited experience, most people receive the baptism with the Spirit at seminars where the Spirit baptism is preached and explained. This sets up a situation where God is ready to confirm His word, and it gives the attendees enough time to deal with any pride or anxiety. Both the seminar leaders and the attendees have come prepared and are exercising faith for people to receive an outpouring of the Spirit. There is no rush; and even if God wanted to delay the release of the Spirit baptism, there is at least an experience of His love among other Christians.

God always keeps His promises. Therefore, do not stop until you have the fullness of the Spirit. This is how we may pray for each other or ourselves:

Lord Jesus, I have repented of my sin, accepted You by faith, and received forgiveness in my (water) baptism; now please allow me to receive the fullness of the Holy Spirit. Fill me. Drench me. Pour out the Spirit on me. Quench my thirst. Amen.

You may want to record your experience after praying this prayer or a similar prayer.

Appendix B

Study Guide

The following study guide can be used for personal or group discussion. May God help you to review the important topics presented throughout the chapters of the book and grow in the understanding of His word. Then, as you exercise faith, I pray that God surprises you with more of the Spirit.

CHAPTER 1

The Word Alone Is Not Enough

(The Holy Spirit Infilling)

Warm-Up

1. What are your expectations as you begin this study?

_____

_____

_____

_____

_____

_____

_____

_____

2. Why do you think the Holy Spirit is often a controversial topic among Christians?

_____

_____

_____

_____

_____

_____

_____

_____

_____

_____

_____

_____

_____

Review of Chapter 1 (Preparation: Read Chapter 1)

Let's Talk About It

Feel free to voice your first impressions in response to Chapter 1. Then tackle the following questions:

1. Read Luke 24:45-50 and reflect on the disciples' knowledge, faith, and worship of God at this point. Do you consider them to be fit candidates for sending out to spread the good news about Jesus? What did Jesus say and why? Read Luke 24:49; Acts 1:4-5,8.

   _____

   _____

   _____

   _____

   _____

   _____

   _____

   _____

2. Does water baptism and the Spirit baptism always coincide? You may look up one or more of the following Bible passages: Acts 8:14-17; 10:44-48; 19:6. According to Acts 2:38-39, what is expected to happen in any person coming to faith in Jesus Christ? What are the different functions of water baptism and Spirit baptism?

   _____

   _____

   _____

   _____

   _____

   _____

   _____

   _____

3. Is the Spirit a person or a substance? See Acts 2:1-4,17-18; Ephesians 2:18; John 16:7-15; and Matthew 28:19.

   _____

   _____

4. What are the three main benefits of your immersion in the Spirit? Identify them in Jesus' own experience of the Spirit baptism: see Luke 3:21-22; 4:1-13,16-21.

_____
_____
_____
_____
_____
_____
_____
_____

What Now?

1. Are you ready to hear more and resist the temptation of jumping to conclusions?

_____
_____
_____
_____
_____
_____
_____
_____

2. If you feel threatened by the teaching on the baptism with the Holy Spirit, can you ask God to turn your fear into a positive hunger for more of Him?

_____
_____
_____
_____
_____
_____
_____
_____
_____

CHAPTER 2

The Bible Describes the Spirit Baptism

Warm-Up

1. How open are you to learn more from the Word of God?

_____

_____

_____

_____

_____

_____

_____

2. How do you feel about going deeper into the things of God?

_____

_____

_____

_____

_____

_____

_____

_____

_____

_____

_____

_____

_____

Review of Chapter 2 (Preparation: Read Chapter 2)

Let's Talk About It

Feel free to voice your first impressions in response to Chapter 2. Then tackle the following questions.

1. What is the baptism with the Holy Spirit? Even before the first disciples were baptized with the Holy Spirit, they had a measure of the Spirit in them, because according to First Corinthians 12:3, "…no one can say, 'Jesus is Lord,' except by the Holy Spirit"—but what more did they receive? The Bible does not offer any definitions, but you may look up one or more of the following Bible passages: Luke 24:49; Acts 1:4-8; 2:2-4; 2:17-21; 10:44-46; 13:52; 19:6.

   _____

   _____

   _____

   _____

   _____

   _____

   _____

   _____

2. Are you baptized or filled with the Holy Spirit? The word "baptism" means immersion and conveys that you are to be submerged in and drenched by the Holy Spirit. Have you experienced this and are you meant to experience this? What do the following Scripture passages suggest? Luke 24:49; Acts 1:4-8; 2:2-4; 2:17-21; 10:44-46; 13:52; 19:6.

   _____

   _____

   _____

   _____

   _____

   _____

   _____

   _____

3. According to Romans 8:14-16, are you meant to have an awareness of the Holy Spirit in your life? Are you always meant to

experience the closeness of the Spirit with you? See Romans 5:5 and First Thessalonians 1:5-7, but also Mark 15:34; Luke 4:1-13; and Second Corinthians 1:8.

_____

_____

_____

_____

_____

What Now?

1. How confident are you that the Holy Spirit assures you of salvation?

_____

_____

_____

_____

_____

_____

2. Are you ready to walk in victory over sin, empowered by Holy Spirit holiness?

_____

_____

_____

_____

_____

_____

_____

3. What steps are you willing to take to expand the kingdom of God and be successful in mission work?

_____

_____

_____

_____

CHAPTER 3

Receiving the Holy Spirit Is for Everyone

Warm-Up

1. What is your most prized possession and how much were you
    willing to invest and sacrifice in order to have it?

    _____

    _____

    _____

    _____

    _____

    _____

    _____

2. How passionate are you about receiving from God?

    _____

    _____

    _____

    _____

    _____

    _____

    _____

    _____

3. How easy is it to receive from God?

    _____

    _____

    _____

Review of Chapter 3 (Preparation: Read Chapter 3)

Let's Talk About It

Feel free to voice your first impressions in response to Chapter 3. Then tackle the following questions:

1. In Acts 8:16-17 the Holy Spirit came after water baptism and with the laying on of hands; but in Acts 10:44-48, the Holy Spirit came before water baptism and without the laying on of hands. Why is there no particular method to follow and then take possession of the Holy Spirit? What does this mean for us?

_____

_____

_____

_____

_____

_____

_____

_____

2. After the disciples were baptized with the Holy Spirit (Acts 2:2-3), they were again filled with the Holy Spirit in Acts 4:31. Like the disciples, you have an ongoing need to be filled and refilled with the Holy Spirit. Are you aware of this dynamic nature of the Spirit's presence in your life? Are you sensitive to the ebb and flow of His movements in your work and worship?

_____

_____

_____

_____

_____

_____

_____

_____

3. How many Christians can receive the baptism or infilling with the Holy Spirit? See Acts 2:38-39 and Luke 11:9-13.

_____

_____

_____

_____

_____

4. One of the spiritual principles that prepares you to receive the Holy Spirit is repentance. How thorough do you think God wants you to be in your repentance? See Acts 2:37-38; Hebrews 12:14; and Luke 14:25-35.

_____

_____

_____

_____

_____

_____

5. Another spiritual principle that prepares you to receive the Holy Spirit is to put your faith in the word of God. Does Acts 19:2 in any way resemble your situation? What do the following passages say about faith and unbelief? Matthew 17:20; Mark 6:5-6.

_____

_____

_____

_____

_____

_____

6. Another spiritual principle that prepares you to receive the Holy Spirit is to pray for the Holy Spirit. Have you ever formulated a prayer for the infilling of the Holy Spirit? What does Luke 11:9-13 teach about such prayer?

_____

_____

_____

7. Another spiritual principle that prepares you to receive the Holy Spirit is to receive the Holy Spirit through the laying on of hands. See Acts 8:17-18; 19:6 and Second Timothy 1:6. Would you be happy to let another Christian serve you in this way?

_____

_____

_____

_____

_____

_____

_____

_____

8. Another spiritual principle that prepares you to receive the Holy Spirit is to wait for the Holy Spirit. See Acts 1:4-5. What could be the benefits of a waiting period before you receive the infilling of the Holy Spirit?

_____

_____

_____

_____

_____

_____

_____

_____

What Now?

1. After what you have read and heard, how much do you still want the Holy Spirit?

_____

_____

_____

_____

_____

_____

_____

2. Are you prepared to spend time, energy, and discipline on the following?

   • One: Repent and completely turn away from everything that you know is wrong in your life.

   • Two: Put your faith in Jesus and trust the promise that you will receive infillings and refillings of the Holy Spirit.

   • Three: Pray for the Holy Spirit.

   • Four: Ask another Christian to lay his or her hands on you and pray for you.

   • Five: Wait for the Holy Spirit to come.

CHAPTER 4

Will You Still Serve Him?
(The Holy Spirit and Suffering)

Warm-Up

1. What makes you truly happy?

   _____
   _____
   _____
   _____
   _____
   _____

2. Do you expect the baptism with the Holy Spirit to be a positive experience for you? In what sense?

   _____
   _____
   _____
   _____
   _____

3. How easy is it to be a Christian?

   _____
   _____
   _____
   _____
   _____

Review of Chapter 4 (Preparation: Read Chapter 4)

Let's Talk About It

Feel free to voice your first impressions in response to Chapter 4. Then tackle the following questions.

1. What were the disciples slow to believe according to Luke 24:25-26? Why do some still have trouble connecting a Spirit-filled life with suffering?

    _____
    _____
    _____
    _____
    _____
    _____

2. What was the problem of the Spirit-filled Corinthians according to First Corinthians 3:1-3 and First Corinthians 13:1-2? How might God confront this problem? See Deuteronomy 8:1-5; Hebrews 2:10; 5:7-9; and Hebrews 12:5-11.

    _____
    _____
    _____
    _____
    _____

3. According to Acts 2:37, why is even our conversion wounding work? Have you ever felt wounded?

    _____
    _____
    _____
    _____
    _____

4. Would you be able to say the same as John Bunyan and the apostle Paul? John Bunyan: "By this Scripture I was made to see that if ever I would suffer rightly, I must *first* pass a sentence of death upon everything that can be properly called a thing of this life, even to reckon myself, my wife, my children, my health,

my enjoyment, and all, as dead to me, and myself as dead to them. The *second* was, *to live upon God that is invisible,* as Paul said in another place; the way not to faint, is to 'look not at the things which are seen, but at the things which are not seen; for the things which are seen are temporal, but the things which are not seen are eternal' (compare 2 Corinthians 4:18)." The apostle Paul: "Far be it from me to glory except in the cross of our Lord Jesus Christ, by which the world has been crucified to me, and I to the world" (Gal. 6:14). How radical is this?

_____
_____
_____
_____
_____
_____
_____
_____
_____

5. Even the Spirit-filled Jesus faced discipline and temptation for forty days in order to bring forth the character that was to handle the power of the Spirit without becoming corrupted (see Luke 4:1-15). What then can you expect from God?

_____
_____
_____
_____
_____
_____

6. What kind of God do you serve? Is He always "soft" with you?

_____
_____
_____
_____

7. At this point of time, are you still passionate about being drenched by the Holy Spirit, or are you losing interest because of the cost involved?

_____
_____
_____
_____
_____

8. Can you count a few of the blessings which have flown from suffering Christians?

_____
_____
_____
_____
_____

What Now?

1. Can you allow God to use suffering in your life to bring forth the character that can handle the power of the Spirit without becoming corrupted?

_____
_____
_____
_____
_____

2. Can you encourage yourself and others to endure patiently?

_____
_____
_____
_____
_____
_____
_____

CHAPTER 5

The Foolishness Continues
(The Manifestations of the Holy Spirit)

Warm-Up

1. What kind of behavior really offends you?

_____
_____
_____
_____
_____
_____
_____
_____

2. Are you aware of any of your own behavior that can be most annoying to others?

_____
_____
_____
_____
_____
_____
_____
_____
_____

Review Chapter 5 (Preparation: Read Chapter 5)

Let's Talk About It

Feel free to voice your first impressions in response to Chapter 5. Then tackle the following questions:

1. How did Jesus offend the people around Him? Are you still offended by any of these actions or circumstances? See John 1:46; Luke 7:34; Matthew 12:24; John 6:61; and First Corinthians 1:18-25.

   _____

   _____

   _____

   _____

   _____

   _____

   _____

   _____

2. What offended people at the very first infilling with the Holy Spirit? See Acts 2:13.

   _____

   _____

   _____

   _____

   _____

   _____

   _____

3. The Bible knows of people falling to the ground in the presence of God (see Dan. 8:17; 10:7-10,15-19; 1 Kings 8:10-11; John 18:5; Rev. 1:17); faces shining supernaturally (see Exod. 34:29-35; Acts 6:15); trances (see Acts 10:10; 2 Cor. 5:12-13); temporary blindness (see Acts 9:8-9) or numbness (see Luke 1:22); trumpet sounds (see Exod. 19:19) and nature phenomena such as smoke and earthquakes (see 1 Kings 8:10-11; Matt. 27:51), lightning and thunder (see Exod. 19:16-19). Among these phenomena and manifestations, is there anything that would offend you? Why?

_____
_____
_____
_____
_____
_____
_____

4. Why would God jeopardize His own work by offending you? See First Corinthians 1:27-29 and Luke 10:21.

_____
_____
_____
_____
_____
_____

5. What are you to do with manifestations? What are the dangers? What can help you in your discernment? See Second Corinthians 11:4; Matthew 13:24-30; Matthew 7:20; First Corinthians 14:40.

_____
_____
_____
_____
_____
_____
_____

6. Based on Jesus' words in Matthew 7:20, "By their fruit you will recognize them," Jonathan Edwards devised five diagnostic questions that help in discerning a genuine move of the Holy Spirit: "1. Does it bring honour to the person of Jesus Christ? 2. Does it produce a greater hatred of sin and a greater love for righteousness? 3. Does it produce a greater regard for Scripture? 4. Does it lead people into truth? 5. Does it produce a greater love for God and people?" How do these questions

put spiritual manifestations into a mature perspective? What is important in matters of salvation? See Luke 24:47 and Acts 2:21,38.

_____

_____

_____

_____

_____

7. In order to receive the fullness of the Spirit, what more could you do in accepting the manifestations of the Spirit and their "foolishness"?

_____

_____

_____

_____

_____

What Now?

1. Can you make a commitment that you will not be offended by God's "foolishness"?

_____

_____

_____

_____

_____

2. Can you allow God to manifest His presence within you in whatever way He chooses?

_____

_____

_____

_____

_____

_____

CHAPTER 6

The Battle Is On
(The Holy Spirit and Spiritual Warfare)

Warm-Up

1. Have you ever been in danger of getting hurt or even killed? What did you do and what did you feel?

_____
_____
_____
_____
_____
_____
_____
_____
_____

2. Are you okay in handling conflict? Are you confident, fearful, resourceful, denying its presence, capable of defusing tension, etc.?

_____
_____
_____
_____
_____
_____
_____
_____
_____

Review of Chapter 6 (Preparation: Read Chapter 6)

Let's Talk About It

Feel free to voice your first impressions in response to Chapter 6. Then tackle the following questions:

1. How much do you and the world believe the following quote by a Christian theologian: "It is impossible to use electric light and the wireless and to avail ourselves of modern medical and surgical discoveries, and at the same time believe in the New Testament world of spirits and miracles…[This is] unintelligible and unacceptable to the modern world."

_____

_____

_____

_____

_____

_____

_____

2. According to the Bible, how central is the conflict with satan to your faith? See Acts 10:38; Luke 22:53; Colossians 2:15; 1 John 3:8.

_____

_____

_____

_____

_____

_____

3. According to the Bible, how central is the conflict with satan to your daily experience as a Christian? See Ephesians 2:1-10; 4:27; 6:12; Second Corinthians 4:4; Acts 26:17-18.

_____

_____

_____

_____

4. Do you live according to the truth of spiritual warfare? Are you aware of engaging the domain of satan in battle? Are you preparing yourself for battle on a daily basis? Do you become vulnerable by downplaying this aspect of your faith and spiritual reality?

_____

_____

_____

_____

_____

_____

5. Why do you need the infilling of the Holy Spirit before you engage in the battle of mission work? See Luke 24:49; Acts 1:8; Acts 10:38.

_____

_____

_____

_____

6. Notice the connection between Jesus' baptism with the Holy Spirit (see Luke 3:21-22), the fight-back of satan (see Luke 4:1-2), and the ongoing battle with satan's domain, rescuing people from his power (see Luke 4:18-19,31-44). What then can you expect to happen after you have received an infilling of the Holy Spirit?

_____

_____

_____

_____

7. How do you explain the events of Mark 1:21-28?

_____

_____

_____

8. What are some of the weapons in spiritual warfare? See Ephesians 6:10-18.

_____
_____
_____
_____

9. How did Jesus use the "sword of the Spirit" in Luke 4:1-13? How did the Spirit-filled Jesus handle His lack of positive emotions and experiences at that time?

_____
_____
_____
_____
_____
_____

What Now?

1. Can comfortable Christians change into Spirit-filled soldiers, engaging the domain of satan in battle? Can you become disciplined?

_____
_____
_____
_____

2. Can you appreciate your need for power and thus seek an infilling with the Holy Spirit?

_____
_____
_____
_____
_____
_____

CHAPTER 7

Speaking in Tongues Is a Gift

Warm-Up

1. What was one of the more embarrassing moments in your life?

_____
_____
_____
_____
_____
_____
_____
_____
_____

2. Is there anything in the church that you find embarrassing or somehow weird? Why?

_____
_____
_____
_____
_____
_____
_____
_____
_____

Review Chapter 7 (Preparation: Read Chapter 7)

Let's Talk About It

Feel free to voice your first impressions in response to Chapter 7. Then tackle the following questions:

1. Have you ever heard anyone speaking in tongues? How did you feel when this happened?

   _____

   _____

   _____

   _____

   _____

   _____

2. How much teaching have you received on the spiritual gift of speaking in tongues before reading this book? Had there been encouragement for you to receive the gift?

   _____

   _____

   _____

   _____

   _____

   _____

3. Is the gift of speaking in tongues necessary for salvation? See Mark 16:16 and Ephesians 2:8.

   _____

   _____

   _____

   _____

   _____

   _____

4. How many Christians received the gift of speaking in tongues in Acts 2:4; 10:44-46; and Acts 19:6?

   _____

   _____

5. Many Christians want to receive all the spiritual gifts, except the gift of tongues. Do you have a similar attitude? Can a resistance to the gift of tongues block a person's baptism with the Spirit (see 1 Cor. 1:25; James 3:1-12; 4:6)?

_____

_____

_____

_____

_____

_____

_____

_____

6. What are some of the uses of speaking in tongues? See Acts 2:11; First Corinthians 14:2-4,13-14,27; and Romans 8:26.

_____

_____

_____

_____

_____

_____

7. Consider the following quotes: "Many people expect to be seized upon, overwhelmed, and virtually compelled to speak in tongues. But this is not the way the Spirit treats us. He leads, He encourages, He prompts, He gives—but He does not force. The prompting may be a syllable, a word, or a phrase in the mind; to the understanding it is a meaningless sound, but when spoken out it leads into a new tongue. Or, it may be a certain 'moving of the Spirit' upon the tongue or lips, which will form into syllables and words as one lends the voice. Or, it may be a spontaneous speaking forth, difficult to describe because it is so personal. People's experience of just how it begins seem to vary greatly. Once begun, however, the phenomenon is fairly consistent: A spontaneous and usually fluent language, in which the words are prompted not by the mind but by the

Spirit." "Once a person has spoken in tongues, he may do so at will thereafter." How do people receive the gift of speaking in tongues?

_____
_____
_____
_____
_____
_____
_____

8. How do you exercise faith and cooperate with the Spirit in receiving the gift of speaking in tongues?

_____
_____
_____
_____
_____
_____

9. What are the two temptations that can diminish the gift of speaking in tongues after it has been received?

_____
_____
_____
_____
_____
_____
_____

10. Is the spiritual gift of speaking in tongues for you?

_____
_____
_____
_____
_____
_____

What Now?

1. Is it now time for you to seek and pray for the baptism with the Spirit?

   _____

   _____

   _____

   _____

   _____

   _____

   _____

2. Can you at the same time ask for the gift of speaking in tongues?

   _____

   _____

   _____

   _____

   _____

   _____

   _____

   _____

About the Author

Edgar Mayer is an ordained minister of the Lutheran Church of Australia and currently serves as the senior pastor of Living Grace in Toowoomba, Australia. He graduated from the Australian Lutheran College in Adelaide and completed doctoral studies in Germany, where he was born. Edgar and his wife, Tatjana, are blessed with two daughters, Dominique and Francisca.

If you would like to contact the author, please write to:
mayeredgar@optusnet.com.au
or visit his website:
www.livinggracetoowoomba.org

Additional copies of this book and other book
titles from EVANGELISTA MEDIA™
and DESTINY IMAGE™ EUROPE
are available at your local bookstore.

We are adding new titles every month!

To view our complete catalog online, visit us at:
www.evangelistamedia.com

Follow us on Facebook
(facebook.com/EvangelistaMedia)
and Twitter (twitter.com/EM_worldwide)

Send a request for a catalog to:

Via della Scafa, 29/14
65013 Città Sant'Angelo (Pe), ITALY
Tel. +39 085 4716623 • Fax +39 085 9090113
info@evangelistamedia.com

"Changing the World, One Book at a Time."

Are you an author?
Do you have a "today" God-given message?

CONTACT US

We will be happy to review your manuscript
for the possibility of publication:

publisher@evangelistamedia.com
http://www.evangelistamedia.com/pages/AuthorsAppForm.htm